THE POWER IN MY WEAKNESS

JACOB MATTHEWS

THE POWER IN MY WEAKNESS

WHISPERS REVISITED

Columbus, Ohio

The Power in my Weakness: Whispers Revisited

Published by Gatekeeper Press
2167 Stringtown Rd, Suite 109
Columbus, OH 43123-2989
www.GatekeeperPress.com

The cover design, interior formatting, typesetting, and editorial work for this book are entirely the product of the author. Gatekeeper Press did not participate in and is not responsible for any aspect of these elements.

ISBN (hardcover): 9781642379051
ISBN (paperback): 9781642379068
eISBN: 9781642379075

CONTENTS

INTRODUCTION

This is a story, a journey through life from the beginning. My name is Jacob and I would like to invite you to enter my thoughts, to walk beside me, to capture my emotions and experience a world not meant to be. This book was born from decades of silence that harbored tremendous guilt, shame, physical, emotional, and sexual abuse, the inability to speak, and the surrender to weakness. I do not pretend to be a writer nor is it my goal to become noticed.

My intent is to make people aware of what goes on in the mind of a child that endures terrible suffering at the hands of others, the very same people that were supposed to be a blessing and a bridge in making the transition into foster care a loving and nurturing one. You do not, however, have to be a foster child to experience these things. There are many scenarios in life that traumatize a child in the same manner whether it involves the rich or poor, young or old, friends or relatives, or sadly, moms or dads.

I grew up in a system that was meant to help unstable families heal. It was intended to be a temporary haven for children while the parents struggled to overcome their difficulties. The hope was for a child to be reunited with Mom and Dad as quickly as possible so the child could then go on to experience a normal and loving family life. This book is not meant to be specifically about a broken system. I know several foster parents in my adult life that are loving and kind to their foster children.

As you continue to read you will discover a deeper understanding of the effects of childhood trauma and how it plays a crucial role in the outcome of lost innocence and self-worth. More importantly, it was written to help others who have suffered connect with my story, to let them know that they are not alone and that I care deeply for them. I pray that they will find forgiveness and peace. We all have a cross; we just want to bury it because it is too painful. My cross has a different meaning now. I have overcome and so can you.

The story opens with the thought process of a very young child, so the wording reflects those thoughts in a childish way. This process matures as the child gets older. Let us begin our journey, a world we will share together from within …

TAKEN

A memory is created when two or more neurons fuse in the brain, giving us the ability to go back and reflect upon our experiences. This process begins before we are born.

I was sitting in my favorite spot on the couch waiting for Dad to come home. It was dark outside as I waited in anticipation. I could smell food cooking, and I couldn't wait to eat. Dad opened the door and tossed me a kaleidoscope. As I gazed into it, I heard rustling sounds coming from the kitchen. Suddenly, there was a loud crash and I dropped my kaleidoscope. I saw a turkey bouncing across the kitchen floor. Dad ran past me with Mom chasing after him. She slashed at him with a shiny knife, and there was red coming out from his arms. I knew what red meant and panicked.

My little mind immediately set my feet in motion to run and get him a towel. Mom disappeared into the night. I was just three and my brother Daniel, a year and a half older, was nowhere to be found and that frightened me. My siblings Warren, Trisha, and Tammy were much older and never around; that was the way things were. I saw them very little. No one was there this night but Mom, Dad, and me.

I went back to the couch and waited. Dad was walking aimlessly around the house, staggering while drops of red followed him wherever he went. He was chanting and stumbling until he fell to the floor. He lay there motionless, finally falling asleep. There was that familiar smell about him. I covered him up with my blanket and went back to the couch. I waited for Mom to come back to help but she never did.

I fell asleep on the couch, where I spent a lot of time. I felt safe there when I was alone. I felt safe there when they were fighting. I felt safe there when they were pushing and shoving. I felt safe there when frying pans flew and dishes broke. In spite of the chaos, I was never touched or hit or beaten. I was held, I took baths, I played, and I slept. I thought I was loved. I thought this was normal.

I woke up the following morning. Dad was no longer on the floor. Mom was in the bedroom and Daniel was lying next to her. She must have slipped back home with Daniel after I fell asleep. I felt better knowing he was home, but my world was about to change. This was when everything started to fall apart.

One afternoon there was a knock on the door and strange people entered the room. Mom, after letting them in, was acting out, talking uncontrollably about Dad and his "friends." I was taken aside by one of the strangers. She looked under my clothes and searched every inch of my body. She asked me some questions that a three-year-old could not possibly answer. "Do you know where Dad is? Are you hungry? When was the last time you ate? Where are your brothers and sisters? Do you hurt anywhere? Does your bum feel okay? Does it hurt when you go to the bathroom? Open your mouth please. Can you please walk over there and back? Where do you sleep? Do you sleep alone?"

Seriously! I loved my mom and dad; that was all I knew. I remembered taking long bubble baths with Mom until the last bubble disappeared. Dad would snuggle with me on the couch late at night, nibbling at my ear. I remembered that smell, and I welcomed it because I knew Dad was with me. What was wrong with lining up cockroaches and playing racing games? Opening the fridge and sipping from a brown bottle was fine with me. Though I was a bit afraid of the jar of pickled pigs' feet, I ate what I ate, and I was happy. If I felt hungry, I didn't know the difference; it was how we lived.

The wobbly toilet seat, searching for toilet paper, faded windows half covered with paper, cobwebs dangling everywhere, the scary clothes washer that caught Daniel's arm right up to the elbow, and the peeling paint all belonged in my little world. The couch, however, was my sanctuary. It felt so soft and dipped in places that would bury my little butt. It had cup holders hanging on the sides filled with used gum, beer bottle caps, cigarette ashes, and pills. Most of my plastic play toys would get swallowed in the bowels of the back cushions. Mom loved to sit with me, and we would try and go into the abyss to find my little trinkets. She would snuggle and sing to me almost every day. She had a beautiful voice; I lived for that. My mom, my couch. Yes, my sanctuary.

The strange people took my happiness from me when they took me away. They separated my brothers and sisters and said they were offering me a chance at a normal life, a life filled with love, compassion, security, and promise. The strange people lied.

I will never forget the moment my mother placed me into the stranger's arms. I had no idea that this would be the last time I would feel the warmth of her body and the gentle touch only a mother can give. She would become a distant memory that still dwells in the shadows of my mind. It would be the same with my dad. The smell of alcohol is the only thing that draws me back to foggy glimpses of a father lost in his own world.

TORMENTING SHADOWS

I was about to turn four and Daniel was with me as we sat in the back seat of the car. I did not understand why I would not be reunited with my other brother and sisters. We were a family. There had been five of us and now we were only two. I was very fortunate however, to have the one brother with me who would eventually play a major role in my salvation. He was a year and a half older than me and a big boy who liked to be mischievous. I was small for my age and a bit shy.

We sat quietly in the back seat just staring out the window, wondering where we were going. We passed the train tracks and the funny-shaped building that we used to hide in after playing chicken with the trains or trying to hitch a ride. We drove by my favorite Aunt Margret's house with the big wraparound porch, the corner store, and then the barber shop with the rotating red and white striped cylinder in the front window. They were all disappearing. The landmarks that once comforted us soon faded away and the car just kept going … and going … and going …

We *finally* slowed and turned onto a long winding driveway. I listened to the sound of stones crunching under the tires as we approached the house. Our first foster house was nothing like our home. The yard was neatly trimmed, the windows were spotless, it was painted pure white, and there was plenty of room to play in the yard. After taking all of this in my eyes turned to the adults standing under a tree in the front yard. They were dressed in dark clothes that blended in with the shade from the tree. I couldn't figure out who was who! The shade seemed to absorb their features. As we started walking towards them I was confused.

Who are these people? I wondered. *Why aren't they smiling? I have to go to the bathroom!*

The strange person introduced us by saying, "It is all right if you call them Mom and Dad."

Why? *I already have a mom and a dad, and I really have to go to the bathroom!*

The stranger left, and my brother and I were led into the house. The father figure guided me to the bathroom as my brother sat on a little white rocking chair in the front room that was surrounded by glass. The bathroom was spotless, no roaches, and the seat wasn't broken. I already missed my broken seat and little insect playmates. The mother figure yelled, "Jacob, make sure you wash your hands."

To this day—and trust me, I am much, much older now—the smell of Dial soap in that bathroom is infused in the neurons deep inside my brain. I would live in the world of foster care for the rest of my childhood, never to return home.

As I left the bathroom, I heard a trembling voice and a snapping sound coming from another room. I began to feel something strange; a profound sense of fear and uncertainty overwhelmed me. I had never felt this before, and I was afraid of what I was going to see. I clung tightly to the wall, bracing myself with my hands as I slid along the way. The woman we had just met in the driveway was standing over Daniel holding a water-soaked dish towel. She repeatedly hit my brother as I stood watching. I had never witnessed anything like this, and I could not move.

I stood there silent, trying to control my emotions. My brother was going on five years old and was helpless, his body fighting every blow. I saw fire and anger in his eyes. He was trying to be strong and resist the pain. When it was over, he was sent to a room. Still I didn't move.

The woman took me by the arm and showed me a broken rocking chair. "See what your brother has done!" I did not understand the meaning behind it because I was just a little boy in total shock, and I can guarantee you that my brother didn't either! We had just arrived, and this was how we were greeted?

All I could think about was my brother. What on earth could cause a person to do such a thing? The father figure just watched without uttering a word. This was not Mom and Dad fighting, something that we were used to and did not fear. We did not fear it because we were never the target; we were the silent observers.

I was so young then. As each day passed, I longed to go home. I no longer felt safe except in my bed. My bed and the darkness became my sanctuary. When darkness came, I knew it would be time for bed soon. I missed every nook and cranny of my couch and imagined that I was back on it. I could dream of my mom singing "You Are My Sunshine" over and over as she held me close. I could smell farina and syrup and damp wood on a rainy day. I remembered the walks by the railroad tracks with my brother and throwing pocketknives at the trees to try and get them to stick. I would wait for Dad on the couch each night anticipating those ticklish nibbles on my ears and his warm breath on my cheeks. These were the memories that gave me hope. I was happy in this world.

Daylight was the enemy. It meant adhering to new rules and structure and brought with it a loss of self-worth, helplessness, and constant fear. A cookie jar is for cookies, and cookies are to be eaten by children, right? Rules applied to the cookie jar. I could hear the water running in the kitchen, and my knees started to shake. She wasn't coming for me; she was coming for Daniel once again. How he could take beatings like that and still stand was beyond me. I hurt just listening to the snapping sounds of the rag. The logic of this one was quite simple: please ask before you take a cookie.

My brother and I came from a place that allowed us the freedom to roam and eat whatever was available, even if it was sometimes a bit scarce. We didn't understand structure. We lived for the moment and had a lot of fun being creative. This home was different. There were endless rules for washing your face, brushing your teeth, clearing your plate, making your bed, and cleaning your room. My brother took beatings so often because he didn't know how to conform to our foster parents demands, nor did I. I felt the sting occasionally but learned from Daniel how to avoid punishment most of the time. God! He was so strong. I would discover just how strong he was as we grew older.

Today, I can't for the life of me remember what these parent figures looked like. All I recall are shadowy figures that moved about the house. The stranger, a little woman wearing high heels with a puffy hairdo, would show up on occasion and talk to them in another room so we couldn't hear what they were saying. I guess it wasn't good because we didn't live in that house for very long. I never understood the stranger. The stranger was the one that moved us around, the one asking all the uncomfortable questions, and the one that ultimately took us away.

What *do* I remember about this place? I remember clean sheets, structure, the smell of Dial soap, Santa Claus with a wire beard lurking about in the basement, Lincoln logs on the kitchen floor, dunking for apples, a plastic horn, but most of all discipline and the snapping sound of that wet rag.

I know what you are thinking: how can a four-year-old remember those details? The answer is simple: a child doesn't forget his home or his real parents. Children need love and security. We didn't get that. There are loving and kind ways to help a child achieve a better understanding of how to behave; constant beatings and living in fear are not one of them.

As I approached six years old, our bags were packed again, we received a hug from the shadowy figures, and we were on our way. We were never given a reason as to why we had to move on. Was it because we were bad little boys?

It was yet another long drive, and I sat quietly, wondering if I would be reunited with Mom and Dad. Where were my other sisters and brother? Funny, they never visited us, but I still believed we were going to be a family again someday.

The stranger that had brought us to our first home was driving the car once again. She talked to us on our way to the new home about the wonderful family in the country we were going to be living with.

THE GIFT

We pulled into the driveway after another ten-sion-filled drive that took so long it seemed like we were driving on a treadmill. I saw a woman. She was short in stature and reminded me of the syrup bottle that was shaped like a woman. From the moment I stepped out of the car, I could immediately sense a warm feeling. I was not frightened of the surroundings.

The woman shaped like a syrup bottle gave Daniel and me a big hug. I hadn't felt a warm hug like that in a very long time. The stranger began removing our stuff from the car and talking to the woman that had just squeezed new life into me. Daniel and I stood there taking it all in. Suddenly, I was met by a boy with bright red hair.

"Hi, I am Rudy, your new brother."

Rudy took me by the hand and led me to the backyard. "You and me are gonna climb this tree." Daniel didn't follow and I could see him still standing by the car as we were sitting in the branches. Rudy said that he was a foster child that had been living with the woman shaped like the syrup bottle since he was a baby. I felt alive for the first time after leaving my real mom and dad.

I would soon find out that there wasn't a father figure in this new house and the woman would be taking care of my brother and me all by herself.

"My name is Loretta," she said, "but you can call me Mom if we want to."

For those of you who have never experienced living in foster care, we use the terms "real mom and dad" or "real brother and sister." It is simply how we communicate what is our true blood and what belongs to others. Daniel and I would often say things like, "Well, this is not our real mom," or, "Why would you call me your brother when I don't even know you? You are not my real brother!" It is difficult to process these things when you are constantly being separated and reunited with strangers. "Am I your real brother, Daniel?" "Yes, Jacob, I am your real brother, don't worry …"

It didn't take long before the word 'mom' felt normal to me. She was so loving and caring. The future brought hugs and kisses and the freedom to do whatever we wanted to do. Homemade food and warmth were ever present. It was a moment in time filled with adventure, joy, and unconditional love from a woman for whom I will forever be grateful. My life in Summersville!

Okay, let's get back to the tree. It was a gigantic apple tree filled with fruit and endless branches that rose above the house. There were others in the backyard that were just as exciting to a little guy with a passion for climbing. The backyard was overflowing with adventure. After we climbed down from the tree, Rudy pointed to a small shack.

"You gotta check this out!" he said. He opened the door to a hole in the ground that smelled like a barn. "Let me show you how to do it. I gotta go anyways."

It was a real outhouse! I had never seen one before, but it was sure neat to be able to drop your drawers in a tiny building and pee down a hole. I learned quickly not to stand next to Rudy. My sneakers were given a quick shower. He laughed and laughed. I joined in; it was funny!

The next thing we checked out was a chicken coop with a funny-shaped roof. "There ain't any chickens. They all died," he said. I guess he wasn't kidding because this chicken coop smelled worse than the outhouse. "Wanna see my fort?"

He took me to the garage that had a ladder in it leading to a loft. We ended up looking out the back window of the loft for hours. Rudy talked nonstop about the lime pile, the woods, the hidden creek, and so much more … All this on the first day; I hadn't even ventured into the house yet! Rudy had me mesmerized, and he was anxious to make me feel welcome.

It was starting to get dark outside, and I began to panic. I was used to the regimen of Dial soap, the sanctuary of my bed, praying that my brother was going to be okay, and yet, I was still outside playing with this curly redheaded boy who had no intention of slowing down. I couldn't help but wonder why the woman shaped like a syrup bottle (Mom from this point on) hadn't called us in. The car that brought us to this place was no longer in the driveway. I decided to venture into the house and look around. Where was my brother?

As I opened the door, I stepped into a room that had dirt on the floor; no, the floor was made of dirt! This room led to the kitchen, and as soon as I entered, Mom picked me up and placed my face over a home-made apple pie. "When it cools, you can have some!" She set me down and took me by the hand, and we began to explore the house. Rudy followed behind while I focused on the surroundings. I couldn't help but notice the dust on the furniture and that things were out of place.

As we passed by the living room window, I saw my brother playing with another boy. "Who is that playing with Daniel?" I said.

"Oh, he lives here too! It is getting late; we need to get moving."

There was a pile of laundry on the bathroom floor (I would later use this as one of my special hiding places). The living room had a worn couch and a little black-and-white TV tucked in the corner. The windows were cloudy, and cobwebs clung to the ceiling. I felt right at home. As we climbed up the stairs, I could hear the wood creaking beneath our feet. My brain absorbed everything around me; every sound, every smell, and whatever my eyes could see.

At the top of the stairs stood a pretty girl. She was much older than me with long flowing hair and bumps on her chest. Her name was Mary. She was Mom's oldest foster daughter. Mom had no real children of her own. I found out later in life that she had never married.

Mary ruffled my hair saying, "He's cute!" and was gone in an instant. I wasn't prepared for what happened next. Mom picked me up, and we took what seemed like an endless walk to the front of the house. A bed was sitting just below an open window in the hallway. She pulled back the sheets, took off all my clothing except for my underwear, and tucked me in. *What! No bath! No soap!*

There was a light bulb dangling just above us. Mom reached up and switched it off. Kneeling beside me, she cradled my hand, gently stroked my hair with the other, and said, "Let's say a prayer: now I lay me down to sleep, I pray the Lord my soul to keep. If I should die before I wake, I pray the Lord my soul to take."

We would say this prayer every night until I left this wonderful place. This prayer connects me to Loretta in ways you cannot imagine. At that time, I had no religion in my upbringing, but I felt something that first night. This beautiful woman shared a gift that would take me through my darkest hours, something that would keep me from breaking or giving up. It was a strength that could only come from above. She gave me a gentle kiss on the cheek as she guided my hand across my chest. She stayed with me until I fell asleep.

Waking up in a new home on the first day was very scary. This home, however, was a gift from above. There was no structure, no regimented daily activity, no shadowy figures or longing to be loved by someone, anyone! I just lay in bed looking at the new surroundings. The long hallway looked much different in the daylight. I couldn't help but notice the cobwebs once again; seeing them made me feel warm inside. I felt a connection with my real home. I wondered why I was allowed to stay in bed and thought I would hop out of bed to do a bit of exploring.

In the hallway, I turned right and entered a bedroom that had two sets of bunk beds. My brother was lying in the lower bed, and above him was Rudy, the boy with the bright red hair. There was another boy whom I had yet to meet sleeping in the bottom of the second bed. It was so good to see my brother safe. I wondered what he was feeling inside and what he was dreaming.

I decided to continue down the hallway. To my left was a bedroom with an old woman lying in bed. I wasn't interested in finding out who she was. At the end of the hallway was yet another bedroom. There was girls' clothing tossed in heaps all about the room. This surely belonged to the pretty girl I had met last night. I decided to ride the banister down the stairs.

The moment I landed on the bottom step, I could smell food cooking in the kitchen. I noticed two beautiful glass doors leading into a large room; I decided that I would explore this room later. I peeked into the bathroom. The bathroom entrance was directly off the living room. I noticed a door exiting from the bathroom at the opposite end, so I followed it to see where it led. This door opened into the basement and yet another door to the outside. I walked down the cellar stairs. There was a crawl space and a partial basement. The smell of that basement, a wonderful damp earthy smell, is still fresh in my mind today.

I climbed back up the stairs and headed into the kitchen. Mom was making bacon and flapjacks. As soon as I entered the room, she picked me up again and put my face over the apple pie. "You missed the pie last night! Go wake your brothers." She set me down, and I ran off. I couldn't wait to wake them up.

Mary wasn't in her bed, and I skipped past the old lady. I woke my brother first. It felt good to wake him. There would be no more pain or the snapping sound of that wet rag. Rudy was next and then the boy in the other bunk bed.

Breakfast was awesome! We could eat as much as we wanted. No portioning or being told to eat everything on your plate. I could see the joy in my mom's eyes as we sat together for our first meal. She officially introduced the boy I had not met the night before as Devon. Devon had a different color skin. He paired off with my brother, and I became glued to Rudy.

Since my birthday was in December, I had just turned six years old. I didn't start school until the next year and it was summer break for the older kids. Because of that, I spent most of my time outdoors from sunup to sundown. I would only go inside to eat, and most of the time, I used the great outdoors as my bathroom; I loved doing that. I remember ants! There were huge black ants that brought back fond memories of playing with roaches. I tried performing the same rituals with these critters as I did when Dad was looking over my shoulder. I soon found out that playing with ants couldn't compare to my old high-speed buddies. Rudy, who was about five years older than me, wasn't about to waste any time watching me play with ants; he wanted me to be his sole partner in exploration and mischief.

Rudy was a regular at a dairy farm that was located four doors down. I was introduced to a large man, Nelson, who allowed Rudy and me to run free over the entire farm. We spent many days at the farm performing little tasks like pushing cow poop down to a conveyor that would load it onto a cart. We would help feed the cows, and occasionally, we tried to squeeze milk. I never got the hang of that, but Rudy was an expert. I loved the smell of the place: poop and fermented silage.

I loved the silo. We would climb to the top and walk the rim on the inside even when it was empty. Can you imagine two little guys walking that rim, hugging the wall just to say we did it without falling? When I think about it today, I know that had I slipped, I wouldn't be typing these wonderful memories. Someone was watching over us. Nelson, by the way, did not know many of the crazy things we did.

We would climb to the top and jump from the top of the silo to the roof of the barn. Fun! Another game was leaping into the silage from the side openings and crawling back out—for hours at a time. And oh, the pitchfork! We had a "stick your foot out and try to see how close it can get to your toes without you moving" contest. Up in the hayloft one day, I told Daniel to play the game and throw me the pitchfork. That was my first trip to the hospital. I still have the round scar on my left knee to this day. I love that scar.

The cows were led out to pasture and kept in place by an electric fence. Red-winged blackbirds would grasp the wires with their feet, die from the electric shock, and swing upside down, remaining attached to the wire. I felt terrible and had many bird funerals in the backyard. Rudy thought I was crazy.

Nelson grew cow corn that he would grind up and put in the silo to ferment. He did this every year to feed the cows. Have you ever run through a cornfield without a shirt on? Anyone who has will never do it again. I was in agony. It was like getting paper cuts on every square inch of your upper body. Rudy thought it was funny. I loved Rudy. He would sometimes play jokes, but he protected me. He loved me as a brother, not as a foster brother. I always felt safe when I was with him.

The tomato plant incident warms my heart when I think about it. Our neighbors planted a garden that had all kinds of vegetables. Rudy planted two tomato plants in our yard, one for me and one for him. I loved my tomato plant. I watched it grow and started to see the green tomatoes blossom. I was so excited! Well, as the days passed, my plant began to die. Rudy could sense my worry, so one night he transplanted a tomato plant from the neighbor's garden to replace my dying plant.

The next day, when I looked at my plant, I saw ripened tomatoes. I knew right away that this wasn't my plant. It wasn't shaped like my plant, did not have the same number of tomatoes, and was much bigger. I was so upset. Rudy admitted what he did because he wanted to make me happy.

The loft above the garage was our special meeting place. One day, we decided to steal all the vegetables from one of our neighbor's gardens and take them up to our bedroom to eat. Obviously, this was Rudy's plan, so I had to go along with it, right? Dusk fell, and we proceeded to pull every vegetable growing next door, roots and all. Rudy and I had two bags each filled to the brim with tomatoes, cucumbers, lettuce, onions, and God knows what else.

Mom was always at home. She was our only parent figure, so she rarely left the house and was always busy cooking. As we walked past her, she asked what was in the bags. I was never good at lying. She saw the look in my eyes and an uneasy feeling in my heart surfaced. Our plan had failed. "Mom, it was Rudy's idea, not mine!" Well, it was true!

We had to go to the neighbors and give them their vegetables back, and Mom bought seeds for the following year. Our neighbor made Rudy bite into a raw onion for his punishment. He bit into it like it was an apple just to spite her. "This is nothin," he said. I was told that I was too cute to be punished. Lucky me! Even so, Mom never yelled, never hit, and never tried to make us feel like we were bad children. With love, she helped us understand the difference between right and wrong.

Richard and Glenda were our next-door neighbors on the other side of the garden. My first encounter with them wasn't very good. Rudy and I "borrowed" some rhubarb from their little field. I think Rudy wanted to see the look on my face when I bit into the stalk. Turns out raw rhubarb isn't very tasty. When the dust settled, I found myself sitting on their front porch drinking ginger ale. These wonderful people took a liking to me. Richard offered me ginger ale and conversation on his front porch every time I wandered into his yard. He would take me to special events that he thought I would like, such as tractor pulls and riding horses. I spent many a day sitting on that porch, sitting on wicker furniture.

Speaking of wicker—Rudy and I had a plan: Let's take a piece of wicker furniture and try to smoke it. "You get it," he said. Well, that was exactly what I did. I broke a piece off and we headed straight for the good woods. The good woods were an awesome place to be. I call them the "good woods" for a very good reason which you will understand later. Sour apple trees were plentiful, and I never stopped eating their fruit. We would climb the trees, sit in the branches, and look out over the landscape for hours.

What goes on inside a little guy's mind is so unique to each individual. I felt like a man when I inhaled that burning wicker. I also got very sick and threw up. I only smoked it once!

Honeybees always fascinated me. One day I was climbing one of the trees in the backyard, and as I looked down, I saw bees coming from the chicken coop. I decided to see where they were living inside. Picking up a big stick, I opened the door to the coop. In the far corner, there was a large round object. Bees were swarming around it, so I decided to be a man and attack their home. I took one swing at the round ball. Honeybees can only sting once; after they sting you, they die. Well, I was stung, and they died.

I picked bees from my shirt, in a lot of pain, but initially thought I was triumphant. Needless to say, I wasn't. Back to the hospital! Thank God I wasn't allergic.

I would have other battles with these enemies. Rudy was the one who ultimately proved the conqueror. Gasoline, a match, a fire … no more bees! Thank God the chicken coop didn't burn. We were so lucky that Mom or our ever-watchful neighbors missed the gigantic gray cloud that wafted briefly above us and was scattered by the wind as we exited the coop. I felt bad for the bees, not liking to see anything die. I brought life to inanimate objects. It didn't matter if it was a toy, the car that I was driving in my neighbors' backyard, or the bird that I was burying. Somehow, in my mind, that bird would fly again because of my special abilities.

The chicken coop had an odd shape to it. It was shaped on an angle, low at one end and high at the other. I could easily get on the roof from the low end and with my legs spread apart, waddle to the top. The top was approximately six feet from the ground. Six feet isn't very high unless you're little, which I was. Each time I closed my eyes and jumped, I felt like I was dreaming. It was like I was in another world for just a bit.

One day Rudy and I were batting stones in the rain, trying to see who could hit the stones the furthest with a stick. Suddenly, I felt a thud on the left side of my head. A warm sensation started flowing down the side of my face. I looked at Rudy, and he looked back at me in horror. "Run!" he said.

Reaching up I felt his stick lodged in my head; it had slipped from his wet fingers as he swung. I pulled it out and ran! And there you have it; just another day with Rudy. This would be my third visit to the hospital. Mom hated the trips to the emergency room. I felt bad for her because I could see the worry on her face. Not only did she worry about our injuries, but she had to explain how we got them. I am not sure which was worse for her.

The lime pile was just beyond our backyard. Farmers used it to fertilize their fields. Lime is white, soft, and feels like a sandy beach. The pile was towering for a little guy. It had smooth, sugary-looking peaks and valleys. It was also fenced in with barbed wire but that didn't stop us, nor did Mom's warning not to go near the place. We would play on the pile and then go up into the loft, get undressed, and shake our clothes out of the loft window to get rid of the lime dust that clung to them (the window faced the back of the yard, so we were safe).

On one occasion, Rudy, Daniel, and I were jumping off the lime pile when the police showed up; yet another phone call from our nosy neighbors! We all scattered. I hid underneath a trailer, Rudy ran off up into the woods, and Daniel ran straight into the barbed wire fence. The barbed wire tore into his neck, and blood was everywhere. I was also discovered, and the police took us back to the house. Rudy was nowhere to be found, of course.

Mom was very angry. She let out a scream "Oh my God! What have you done this time!" Mom *never* yelled. I think it was mostly because she had to make yet another trip to the hospital! My brother had a scar that ran from just below his chin to his upper chest. Many years later, in another chapter of our lives, when I would see my brother, I'd always look at his neck. The scar that gave him pain brought me comfort because it would bring me back to a time in my life that was so brief and so wonderful.

On another day, we were once again jumping and playing in the lime pile. We didn't notice that it was starting to sprinkle. The sprinkles then turned into a downpour. For those not in the know, it's wise to stay away from a lime pile when it's raining. We were on top of the pile, and by the time we reached the bottom, it was like trying to wade through a muddy sandpit. Rudy and I made it to the edge, but Daniel was stuck up to his knees. I thought he was a goner. It was like something you would see in the movies. Grab the stick and pull!

I was so happy when he made it to the edge. His feet were bare; he had lost his shoes, never to be recovered. We let the pouring rain wash away the evidence that was clinging to our bodies, but Daniel had to figure out a way to explain how he had lost his shoes. I don't remember how that one was resolved. All I remember is that I was in the clear and my brother was safe.

When I was little, I loved the way the rain felt when it touched me. I loved the smell of it. One of my favorite things to do was to sit in my neighbors' car that was rusting in their backyard. I would sneak over and sit in the driver's seat pretending to drive. I felt safe inside the car. The sound of the rain hitting the windshield and the metal roof was so relaxing. I would sit there for hours pretending to be the grown-up. I would roll the window up and down, adjust the mirrors, honk the horn, and press on the gas pedal. Though I could barely see over the steering wheel, that didn't matter. I could take my car anywhere and still feel safe at home. While Rudy was in school I spent a lot of time on my own. The car was a great place to pass the time.

I am typing what pops into my head. There is no specific order of events now. These thoughts continue to bring me happiness even today. What took place in this tiny little town allows me to open a window in my mind for you to see the only time in my life that I truly felt peace in my heart. It was a special peace, one that cannot be replicated because of the childhood memories that will soon be revealed to you.

Let's keep going. Okay, so I had time on my hands when Rudy was at school. I decided to do a little research on what Mary looked like naked. What? Can't a little guy be curious? I figured out that when Mary thought no one was in the house, she would leave the bathroom door open. My plan was to hide behind the couch that was located near the bathroom entrance. Remember when I said that the bathroom was off the living room? Perfect spot to peek! The problem was that I had to pick the right time. The right time lasted forever, and I was about to give up.

Mary finally showed up and started the bath water. When the water stopped, I could see clothing flying in front of my eyes and landing on a pile of clothes, but no sign of a naked Mary. I waited until she was finished to see if I could get a glimpse, but to no avail. Oh well, I tried. I wasn't about to give up; that pile of clothing could easily hide a sixty-pound little boy.

The next day, I lay in wait. I was so excited because I was completely covered from sight. My little eyes closed when she entered the room. I could hear the water running, the clothes landing on top of me, and the sound of Mary slipping into the tub. My eyes slowly opened, and there was Mary; all I could see was the top of her head. I was thinking that maybe I could crawl out of the bathroom without her seeing me. Instead, I chickened out and lay stiff as a board under all those clothes.

Well, it happened. Mary got out of the tub and stood right in front of me. She certainly did not look anything like my mother! What went through my mind, you ask? I saw a naked girl, and that was enough for me. Mission accomplished, and I couldn't wait to tell Rudy. I had planned it all on my own, and I thought he would be proud of me, and he was. It didn't end there, however. He had to have his part in it. What did he do?

When Mary was taking a bath one day, he told me to put my ear up against the door to listen and then pushed me in. I saw her lying butt-up in the tub; that was my reward for doing something without telling him first. Yes, she screamed, "Get the hell out of here!" and Rudy had the last laugh. By the way, I already knew girls didn't have a penis; my mom taught me that.

I loved the Mickey Mouse club! I would sit in front of the little black-and-white TV waiting for the show to start so I could join in on the song. One day, while waiting for the show to start, there was a funeral parade on every channel. I was so upset! Mom tried to explain to me that the president had died. I couldn't grasp what she was saying. All I wanted to do was put on my ears and sing. I never forgot that.

We had several cats and a dog. While I was playing in the kitchen one day, I backed up onto an open can of dog food. The metal lid sliced into the tendon on the back of my left foot. Blood was everywhere, and I was, for the first time in all my hospital visits, in a lot of pain. It took a long time for the injury to heal, but I never slowed down when it came to having fun. My antics were typical of a boy who was loved and well cared for back in those days. Children nowadays don't have this. Parents today worry more and have reason to do so. I guess I can consider myself very lucky to have experienced so much freedom in a world so uncertain.

Our cats had kittens all the time, and we would give them away. One night, a kitten was eating food from the dog dish. The dog grabbed it by the head and flung it across the kitchen floor. The poor thing was bleeding badly, and I was so upset. Rudy took the kitten out to the backyard and shot it in the head with a BB gun to put it out of its misery. I didn't speak to him for a long time. Back then that was the thing that people did; it was not something out of the ordinary. Try doing this today and see what happens. Of course, I had my little kitty funeral.

There was a shopping trip incident. Mom took Rudy, Devon, Daniel, and me shopping when Mary wasn't available to keep an eye on us. I loved riding anywhere in her car, but when it came to shopping, I wasn't overly enthusiastic. As soon as we arrived in the parking lot, Devon had to go to the bathroom. As we entered the store, Mom immediately began the search for the little boys' room. Devon was in a panic. He didn't look very well and was clutching his stomach, complaining that "it hurts." We finally reached our destination, and Mom sent Rudy in with Devon. Rudy came back out and asked Mom for some money. I decided to go in to see what was up. The bathroom stall was coin operated, and you had to pay to use the toilet!

As you already know, I was a tiny person. I tried to shimmy under the stall door to get inside to open it. This thing was like Fort Knox! There was no getting under it or over it. The only way to enter was with a turn of a coin-filled slot. By the time Rudy came back, it was too late. Poor Devon couldn't hold it any longer. Mom came in and tried to clean him up as best she could. She threw away his pants and underwear and wrapped his lower body in a clear plastic bag. I felt terrible because I couldn't help.

As Mom was walking back to the car with Devon cradled in her arms, all I could think about was the drive-in movie that my real dad took me to when I was younger. In the movie, a man was carrying a naked body wrapped in a clear plastic bag. The lady was placed in the trunk of a car and pushed into a swamp. That scene was the only part of the movie that I could remember at the time. I will let you figure out the title. Devon was put in the back seat of the car, and with the windows wide open, we all had a not-so-pleasant ride back home.

I am just going to keep going with my thoughts …

I used to dream a lot when I was young and still tend to today. Sometime after moving in to this wonderful place, I had a dream about my real mother. I hadn't seen or heard from her or my real dad since I was taken away and placed into foster care. For some reason, the dream unfolded in the cellar where Rudy and I played a lot. It was a great place to play hide-and-seek or commando crawl in the crawl space. We would build things like a German tank made from a wine barrel, a rubber tire, and four rusted wheels borrowed from undisclosed locations. We would squeeze helpless toys in a vise, hammer, screw, or nail anything we could get out hands on. It was a fun place, and as I said before, I loved the smell. Why then would I have such a bad dream that relates to the cellar? It is just how our dream world works. Sometimes, it is way out there …

In the dream I was standing in the cellar with items of all shapes and sizes strewn around the place. As I looked at the back wall, it opened to reveal an ocean without any landmarks, as far as the eye could see. A helicopter came into view and hovered high above the water. The doors slid open, and I could see my real mother bound tightly with rope from head to toe. She was pushed out of the doors and fell slowly toward the water below. I panicked and tried to reach her before she hit the water because I knew she would drown. Every step I took was met with an obstacle. I watched as she fell closer and closer to the water. No matter where I turned, I couldn't move. I had to keep watching as she entered the water. *Why isn't Dad helping her?*

The helicopter moved out of view, and the splash from where she entered faded away to a smooth, shiny surface. Silence. She was gone.

I had this dream for many years, even as a young adult. It played out the same way every time. This dream would be just one of many topics discussed in therapy as I tried and continue to try to deal with the hidden demons that plague me. These dark secrets will be revealed to you as we continue to travel this journey together. Not just yet though. Please let me stay for just a little while longer in this world. I am shaking; I need to stop for a bit. I am sorry.

I'm back. Remember the old lady I mentioned seeing when I first moved in? She moved into the living room area and spent many days lying in bed, barely moving or uttering a sound. There were tubes dangling everywhere. I soon realized the sadness in my mom's eyes was because this poor woman was her mother. I never thought about the connection until she became ill. One day, Mom was standing over her for a long time; I could sense that something was very wrong. She stood there holding her mother's hand, crying deeply; she had passed away. I had never seen Mom cry before, and all I could do was stand next to her holding her dress. She looked down at me and said, "Please go outside and play for a little while. Mom needs to be alone for a bit."

The next three days were so eerie. Mom's mother lay overnight in a coffin in that room with the beautiful glass doors. The funeral was held in our home! All I can remember about the funeral was that everything was black. It was good to see Mom smiling once again when it was over. I didn't go into the room with the glass doors for a while after that. It's funny how things were handled not so long ago.

There was a pond across the street that sat at the bottom of a long sloping hill. This place was awesome. It was filled with all sorts of creatures. Rudy and I would spend hours and hours trying to catch anything that moved. We managed to catch a painted turtle that we brought home to try and keep as a pet. For some reason, it didn't matter what we brought home—a turtle, frog, toad, crayfish, catfish, rabbit, baby birds, mice, neighbors' pets, or any other living creature; they all met with the same fate. The grass always looked great in the backyard.

Another place I loved was the culvert! This was a place that I would go to when I was alone, and my brothers were in school. This sanctuary was nestled between the woods and the lime pile. I would crawl underneath and watch the pollywogs slowly morph into frogs. There were cattails and milkweed everywhere. I loved opening the cattails and breaking the milkweed to see the white stuff ooze out onto my tiny fingers. The water flowed over my toes and a sip to quench my thirst made me feel like I was in control of everything around me. Once again, it was my domain, and it belonged to me.

I loved this world. I controlled it. In my mind, these things belonged to me. When a car or truck drove over the culvert while I was underneath, I felt protected; nothing could hurt me, and I was king. I didn't even want my partner in crime to invade this space. It was mine and mine alone.

It was a Sunday morning. I never really had any thoughts about church. Mom and I would say our nightly prayer, and that was about it. One Sunday morning I was pulled from my usual slumber and coaxed into taking a bath. This was highly unusual. Mom dressed me up in clean clothes, looking like a little man wearing what she called "church" shoes instead of sneakers. I had never worn shoes like that before. Mom gave me a slice of toast with my favorite grape jam, and out the door we went.

"Okay, everyone, line up." Mom made sure that everyone was accounted for before we left the porch. As we were walking, she started to tell me about the place that we were going. She talked nonstop about a man named Jesus, the cross, and what a sin was. I was mostly concerned about the sin part because if it was true, I was in big trouble!

The church was about two miles away from our house. Little people have little strides, and my legs and feet were on fire. I didn't let Mom know because I wanted everyone to think that I was invincible, and nothing could stop me. Thank God (no pun intended) we reached the church before I broke down into tears. It was a bit spooky at first sight. There were graves on the front, sides, and back of the church. When I entered and saw Jesus hanging from the cross, I felt so sorry for him. I didn't have much of a grasp on what Mom was saying on the way except for the sin part. Seeing Jesus, big as life, nailed to a cross was terrible. Mom said that he died for me to save me from my sins.

We sat in the pews and went through all sorts of rituals. I paid little attention to them. Instead, I stared at the cross most of the time wondering if the red stuff on Jesus' body was real blood. When we left the church and started our journey home, Mom asked me what I thought about meeting Jesus. I said, "He is a nice man and I don't like Him hanging on the cross. Is that real blood, Mom?" She picked me up, gave me a big hug, and said that Jesus loved me. I felt good inside even though I had no idea that she was setting me up for that gift, the gift I would find later in life. Words cannot express just how beautiful a person Mom was. *I do know this:* she is with Jesus today.

I enjoyed going to church after that. It grew into a regular Sunday morning event since Mom didn't have to worry about caring for her mother anymore. The little glass cups filled with grape juice and the tiny pieces of bread, the plays (I was a little drummer boy), the long walks, and conversation with Mom. All were wonderful! Thank you, Lord, for those moments in time. I love you!

The Wizard of Oz: this would be my first encounter with the story of Dorothy, the Wicked Witch, and the great Oz. Mom sat me down alongside Rudy and gave us a plastic vine with cherry-shaped gum attached to the branches just before the movie started. I loved picking the gum from the branches with my teeth; one of my favorite treats. It seems so strange to me as I type this that I do not remember my brother being around me; most of the time, I was always with Rudy. I would have liked to have gotten to know Daniel better while in this home. I had no fear of him being attacked, and that was great, but today, I am saddened by the fact that we didn't connect having fun together. Our bond would be strengthened in the next home in a much different and horrifying way. I never really got the opportunity to know my brother outside of the abuse and humiliation that we endured.

Sorry, I stray a bit when I am thinking. Back to Oz. Do you remember the first time you saw it? I was scared out of my pants! Rudy had his usual fun making me jump and scream when the Wicked Witch or those flying monkeys popped up on the screen. Everything was in black and white back then, so it made some of the scenes appear to be more intimidating to the viewer. I could see Mom having a laugh as well; I thought she was on my side, and she was. She would nudge Rudy when the scary parts were on. I think it was to let him know to be gentle. He had so much energy; he never slowed down. Every time I think about him, I feel good inside. I was so lucky to have him as a constant playmate. When he scared me, made me do things that got me in trouble, gave me a toy that belonged to the neighbors, or woke me up in the middle of the night to go on adventures, it was all because he loved being around me, keeping me safe and taking care of me. *The Wizard of Oz* was a fun night!

The loose-tooth incident was a classic. I had a loose tooth that I made the mistake of showing Rudy. "Look, I can wiggle it with my tongue." I know what you are thinking, and yes, that's exactly what happened! He tied a string to my tooth, attached the string to the bathroom doorknob, and slammed the door. It worked the first time.

The marshmallow-toss incident was kind of disgusting when I think about it, but it was certainly a memorable challenge! Remember the room with the bunk beds? Well, there was this huge tin can that we placed in the far corner of the room. While it wasn't something that we would normally do, Rudy and I peed in it one night because we were too lazy to go downstairs. A couple of nights later, Mom gave us a large bag of pink marshmallows; I hated the way they tasted.

The evening was special because the game involved all four of us. We piled on the top bunk and were each given a marshmallow. Rudy oversaw distribution of the nasty edibles that Mom had given us. The object of the game was to see who could toss the marshmallow into the tin can from where we were sitting. If the marshmallow made it into the can, you were given the choice of eating a marshmallow or forcing someone else to eat one. If you missed, you had to eat one. Rudy went first (obviously) and landed it right inside the urine-filled tin can. Yes, I had to eat one! It was my turn, and I missed; I had to eat another. You get the picture? Daniel and Devon were pretty good at force-feeding me those disgusting pink marshmallows, and when the game was over, I wasn't feeling very well.

It took a while before Mom noticed the smell. Can you imagine walking up to a tin can filled with urine and pink marshmallows floating in it, not to mention the ones that missed? Oh well, I think she knew who was behind it. Mom didn't yell; she just told us it was wrong like she did many times before. She was amazing!

Maple syrup season was one of our neighbor's favorite time of year. Nelson, the dairy farmer, owned a lot of land. Just beyond the electric fence at the south end of his field, there were endless rows of maple trees. He had an amazing network of tubes and buckets that would collect the sap from the trees. I loved this time of year too. The amount of sap that the trees gave up was incredible. Buckets and buckets were hauled to the small building next to the barn and dumped into a large vat. The sap boiled for a long time before the sweet smell of syrup emerged.

It takes a tremendous amount of sap to get just a little bit of syrup. I would wait anxiously for the first sip. Nelson would dip his ladle in the boiling vat, pour some into a small glass, allow it to cool, and then give it to me. "Make sure you blow on it and sip it slow," he said. He never got it wrong. The taste was out of this world. Mom always got free maple syrup. I can still taste it today: maple syrup and flapjacks; what a life back then!

There was an old man that lived across the street and several doors down. He was a kind, quiet person who spoke in a whispering voice. I felt sorry for him because he lived alone and rarely had visitors. Occasionally, I would walk back and forth in front of his house waiting for him to come out and sit down in his oversized rocking chair on the porch. I must admit that I was hoping for more than just casual conversation. He would sometimes invite me in and offer me a chocolate bar. I can still remember the strange, stale smell of the inside of his house. The chocolate-bar wrappers smelled just like it, but that never stopped me from eating them.

When the man spoke, I enjoyed listening to his soft voice. I could tell that my presence made him feel good, and I would listen to his stories for as long as I could. He would often repeat the same stories over and over. I would try and react like it was the first time that I had heard them. He passed away not long after my first summer. I cried when he died; he was a good friend.

As time passed, while my brothers were in school and I no longer had the old man to bother, I would venture further away from my nest. I enjoyed crossing the street and exploring the neighbors' yards. There was a white house on a corner lot with a roadway next to it that rolled downhill at a steep angle.

The backyard of this house was contoured the same way. One day, I was rolling down the backyard with my arms held tight to my body. When I reached the bottom and stood up to try and see if I could walk without falling over, I stumbled into a chubby boy wearing a black mask. He said, "My name is Kevin Smith" and added that he had just moved into the house at the top of the hill. He was the same age as me but much bigger. He asked me if I wanted to play Batman and Robin (now the mask made sense).

I had to make a minor adjustment if we were to play: "Only if I can be Batman!" Well, we played Batman and Robin almost the entire summer. Can you imagine what we must have looked like, Robin being almost twice the size of the Caped Crusader? Our adventures, however, abruptly came to a halt as soon as Rudy came home from school. Kevin was no match for Rudy; nobody was. When Rudy entered the picture, he wanted me and only me. I loved that!

Oh no! Back to the hospital, but this time it wasn't me. Daniel had just come home from school. We usually entered through the back of the house (the room with the dirt floor). Rudy and I had plenty of homemade objects that were filled with nails. Daniel tripped coming in, and when he stood up, there was a board with a nail that went straight through the palm of his hand and stuck out the other side. I thought I was going to die! Mom was there when it happened and witnessed the whole thing.

I was amazed at how my brother reacted. He calmly grabbed the board and pulled the nail back through his palm. He looked at us and said, "I bet you guys would cry like babies." I know I would! Mom was white as a ghost. Rudy, on the other hand, couldn't stop laughing. He was always laughing at our misfortunes.

All I could think about was why he wasn't crying! Can you imagine a nail going through your palm all the way to the other side and not even crying? I guess it was all those painful past experiences that allowed him to block it out.

When the day finally came, I was all hyped up for school. My first day was wonderful! We had probably a good three-quarters of a mile to a two-room school that went all the way up to eighth grade. The bathrooms were outhouses that were built into the school. My teacher's name was Mrs. Herman. She took a liking to me right away. I may have been the littlest guy in class, but thanks to Rudy, I wasn't quiet or shy anymore. Actually, I was a bit of a troublemaker.

I remember one day, we were at recess, and there was a box of toys for us to play with. I found a set of boxing gloves, put them on, punched my brother in the face, and knocked one of his teeth out. Scared, I ran out of the school and straight home to Mom. Daniel stayed at school and thought nothing of it. He was so tough! The next day, I was told to sit in the corner for the day. They did those things back then. I would sit in that chair many a day, but Mrs. Herman still favored me. She gave me a book called *I Made a Line*. It was a funny rhyme book. I remember bits like "an eye on a fly on a frog on a log." I held on to that book for a long time.

I loved recess. Kevin and I still played Batman and Robin. We would also fight to see who could ring the recess bell. I made other friends too. There was a boy named Bobby, who was almost completely deaf. He wore a hearing aid that would sometimes make noises. I remember one day, I was sitting behind him and threw a pencil at him. It landed right in the crease of his ear as though he placed it there himself. The entire class was in an uproar, and I automatically moved to my spot in the corner.

School was great for the holidays too. We would paint crazy scenes on all the exterior windows for Halloween, Thanksgiving, and Christmas. We would perform little plays and sing songs. I remember playing a rusty bell. I could go on forever talking about school antics, but the time is drawing near; my childhood innocence is about to disappear. There is no way to express what I am feeling right now. I wish I could stay in this world, but that is not God's plan.

My second Halloween did not go as I had planned it. I would be eight years old in a couple of months. At this age, I was anticipating dressing up as a scary monster or superhero. But I was a cute little blond-haired boy with a very small frame and my mom had a much better plan for me. I was excited to find out what costume she had in mind. She started with the face makeup. I was thinking how cool I was going to look because she spent a lot of time on my face. The next thing to go on was a pair of white tights. Okay, heroes wear tights. Then came the wig; um, do heroes wear wigs? The final touch was a white fluffy dress! "Mom please, no!"

I was the cutest little girl on the block. I would never be able to live this one down. I did get a lot of compliments and a boatload of candy though. Mom was in her glory and loved every minute of it. When I look back on it now, I am glad it made her feel good inside.

I am sorry but I continue to get sidetracked. I had a dream last night that I need to share. I was in the foster home that I have yet to explore with you. My foster father was sick and in bed. He was yelling at me for something that I may have done; I am not quite sure. Strange, too, was that I was just a child. As I approached him, I could see that he was completely covered and huddled between clean white sheets. As I drew the covers back, I saw a frail body, still very angry at me but weak and in pain. I thought of nothing but to try and comfort him and to ease his suffering.

Behind me was my real mother. She was so beautiful and young-looking. She watched me as I tried to help this man. The last vision I had of my mother while she was alive was that of a person who was not in touch with reality. She was old and stared at the end of the cigarette she was smoking, watching the tip of it glow as she inhaled. She would do this for hours on end, sitting and mumbling about how Satan was constantly after her. This dream brought her back to the person I dreamed of as a child.

When I awoke, I felt good inside; I had seen my mother. She was young, beautiful, spoke in a loving manner, and was normal. I had helped a man that you will eventually meet and who was part of a childhood nightmare, yet I still felt good inside. Was this God's way of telling me that I needed to forgive? Did He place my mother in the dream to help me? Yes, He did.

My mind is stalling, preventing me from moving on. It is trying to stop me from opening the vault that contains my secrets, the vault to which only I hold the key. I find it difficult to breathe or type or think. I protect it. I fear it. I am afraid to open it. I find myself crying a lot lately out of the blue. I cry when I am alone where no one can see me or hear my thoughts. My mind is telling me to leave it alone; it can't hurt me now. But the truth is that the vault is never completely sealed. This is why I am writing this book. I need to let others know that they are not alone.

I share a bond with some of you readers that only we can understand. We go about our daily lives as though nothing is wrong. We strive to fit in, to be normal, to have relationships that won't fail, to be loved and feel secure, and to hold down a good job. This vault will not allow it. It will not allow our minds to ever have true peace. I am hoping and praying that if I open it up and release all its content onto these pages and continue to share my story, we will find peace together.

I could go on living in Summersville. It is in a place that I protect because I never want to lose it or forget that it existed! It was a real place in time, and I will cherish it forever. But the time has come to open the vault.

It was shortly after my second Halloween that I noticed something was wrong. Mom was talking a lot to my caseworker. She was sad and uneasy. I will never forget the sadness in her face when she sat me down to tell me that I had to leave. She was crying and said that I was going to a new home. She said that my brother was going too and that we would be okay. She said that we would be well taken care of in our new home and that my brother and I would be happy.

As each day passed, I became more and more anxious. Mom was gathering up all our belongings and packing them in boxes. After seeing this, I knew that I didn't have much time left. I wish I had known why I was leaving; I was a good little boy. We were never given an answer. Knowing why we were taken away from this wonderful place might have helped calm the unsettled feeling inside of me that is still with me to this day. Was it because they wanted to reunite us with more of our real family? If that was the reason, it didn't work. We would be separated even more as we continued to navigate through this system.

I started to wonder what the new home would be like. Would I have another foster brother like Rudy? Would I have a mom and a dad? The thoughts of my real parents came rushing back. I wished that I could see them. I wished that I could go home and be with them. I never saw my real parents while I was in this home either; where were they? I still loved them! I hadn't forgotten them! Had they forgotten about us? I guess they were not ready to take us back yet. Maybe someday.

The caseworker was standing by her car in the driveway. The bags and boxes were at the door, and Mom was in tears. None of my foster brothers or Mary were around to see us off. I am sure Mom planned it that way. As they were loading the car, my mind was racing; this wasn't real. I was dreaming. I was going to wake up and be safe in my bed. It was that same feeling I would get when I jumped off the chicken coop roof. I lost it as soon as Mom put her arms around me and kissed me. I was hoping she would never let me go. Instead, she led me to the car and put me in. "I love you. I will always love you!" she said. Then she turned and walked away.

I would not see or hear from her until I was a grown man when I returned to see her once. I wanted to recapture just for a moment, maybe a few hours, what I was never able to get after I left her. As I am pressing down on these keys, I still don't have it. I am sixty-one years old and have lived my life without reattaining what she gave me. Those who know me today, even my children, will never understand this. I would visit the two-room school on occasion, and drive by the house, but that wonderful feeling of childhood peace, love, and security would forever be just beyond my reach.

THE BIRTH OF A NIGHTMARE

Daniel and I sat quietly in the back seat once more. I remembered what it was like when I left Mom and Dad, when I left my second home, and now this, my third. Would my fourth home be my last? Would I ever be back home with Mom and Dad? I thought about Rudy and how much I was going to miss him. This trip was just like the last; it seemed like we were never going to stop moving around. When you have no idea where you are going, time lingers on.

As we approached the new home, I noticed that all the houses were close together. I wasn't used to this. It sat on a corner lot with a fenced-in yard that wrapped around most of the house. The yard looked unkempt and weeds were choking in the fence. The curtains were drawn shut and most of the backyard had poured cement from the curb to the foundation of the house; no grass. I immediately began to feel sick inside. Something about this house frightened me.

There was no one to greet us in the driveway. We were brought to the door, and the caseworker—yes, the stranger finally had a name I could identify with—knocked. It was getting dark at the time, and it was cold outside.

As the door opened, a tall, thin woman with a smile that didn't seem normal stepped back to allow us to enter. There were three children of different ages staring at us. They were all boys. The little one was cute, with light brown hair. The middle boy was good- looking, also had light brown hair, smiled a lot, and was focused on Daniel. The oldest boy however, made me tremble inside. He had black hair, was tall, chubby, and seemed different than the other two. The caseworker brought our belongings in and spoke to the woman for several minutes and then turned and left.

My brother and I just stood there not knowing what to do. The woman looked at us and said, "You can call me Janet, Mrs. Peters, or Mom." I didn't call her anything for a very long time.

We were told to put our belongings in a room upstairs, escorted by one of the children, and to come back down to the kitchen. I was shaking all over. Her voice was not that of a loving mother figure. The sound coming from her lips echoed loudly. Every word she spoke heightened my senses. There was no escaping its grip on the reality of the situation.

When we arrived back in the kitchen, there was a stool set up in the middle of the room. "Jacob, take your shirt off and sit on this stool." I did as she asked without hesitation. My mind was flooded with thoughts of our second home. I had learned back then that if I did what I was told, I would be okay; unfortunately, I would discover that this didn't hold true in this world.

She took out a shaver and proceeded to cut all my hair off. I asked, "Why are you doing this?" She did not say a word. When she finished, she told me to stand in one spot and not to move.

My brother was next. I was surprised that he did as he was told. I am certain it was because he was frightened too. I had never seen him tremble like that before. I moved just a bit and she said, "Don't move. Stand where I told you to stand!"

I could not feel my legs; it was the same feeling I had when I first saw my brother being whipped. I was dying inside, and I wanted to be back where I came from. All this time the three children were watching, amused, each with the same look of anticipation and excitement on their face, wondering what would happen next.

When this woman finished with my brother, she marched us up to the bathroom. I was told to take off my clothes while this woman (I will refer to her as Janet from this point on) started running the bath water. As you are aware by now, all my body parts were tiny. I stood silent, trying not to move, with my hands cupped over my private parts. My brother stood next to me and began removing his clothes.

We were told to get in the water. It was cold and shallow. The water barely covered our legs. She gave us orders as to what to do to get ourselves clean. When we were finished, we were told to get out and dry off. We again stood naked, shaking, waiting for clean clothing. I kept my hands in front of me.

When the clothes finally arrived, we got dressed, and I was given the first of countless chores. "Jacob, clean the bathtub!" Her voice frightened me so much that I jumped into action even though I didn't have a clue as to how to clean it. I could sense that she was very pleased with my reaction. She escorted Daniel back to the kitchen, where he was told to stand in one spot; I would join him soon after.

My brother and I looked at each other. We were almost bald, clothed in pajamas that weren't ours, and unable to speak. Within a few short hours, we had lost our freedom to even move within the house. We lost the freedom to speak without first being spoken to. We were stripped of our dignity and could barely recognize each other. Thoughts of darkness and bedtime came flooding back. I would be safe in bed, I thought, and prayed that I would be there soon.

The children were watching something on the television that was set up in the eat-in kitchen area. My eyes and ears turned to the TV when I heard the Red Baron singing a song to Snoopy. Janet looked at me and said, "Take this folding chair to the basement and put it at the bottom of the stairs." The basement stairs were located off the kitchen. As I was picking up the chair, I glanced over to look at the TV. My face was suddenly burning, and I felt dizzy.

Janet had slapped me across the face and said, "Do as you are told." I made it to the bottom of the stairs and set the folding chair down, and as I was ascending the staircase, she told me to sit on the top step.

I sat down; she turned off the basement lights and closed the door, and there I was, in complete darkness. My face was on fire, and I was now a prisoner. I sat on that step for hours. My bottom was numb, and I rocked constantly from side to side to try and get feeling back. I begged to go to the bathroom, but no one answered. I would soon discover that this was one of Janet's favorite tactics to inflict physical pain and gain control. I had no idea what happened to my brother.

The basement door finally opened. I could barely stand or move and wasn't fast enough for her. Janet grabbed my arm and dragged me into the light. By the time my eyes adjusted to the brightness, I was standing in front of the toilet. I was told to sit on the toilet and go. She just stared at me as I sat there. I tried so hard to go, but it wouldn't come out. Some of you have experienced this, right? When you hold it for so long, it sometimes takes a while for your body to open things up again.

I could see that she was getting mad so I thought if I started crying, she would feel sorry for me. Big mistake! "I said hurry up!" I felt the sting once again; now my crying was justified.

I was pulled from the toilet and taken up to another level of stairs and told to get in the top bunk bed and go to sleep. As I lay there, I cried quietly, longing to be with my mother and Rudy. I knew in my heart that that day would never come. I no longer felt safe, not even in the darkness and under the sheets, not in this house. I thought about my parents again. Why hadn't I seen them? Did they even know where I was? Did they no longer love me?

The next morning, I was awakened by the oldest boy and escorted down to the kitchen where I was soon joined by my brother. We were told to sit and eat. The milk didn't seem like milk, and the cereal was round and tasteless. Later on I learned it was powdered milk—just add water. Yuck! My mind was still in shock from what had happened the night before. I closed my eyes and prayed that I was dreaming. I wanted to jump off the chicken coop and be free from this nightmare. When we finished eating and put the folding table and chairs away, we were back in the kitchen. Janet opened the basement door and pointed. "Jacob, sit."

I was back on the basement stairs with the door closed. My brother was somewhere else. It was early morning, and I couldn't help but wonder why I was once again on the steps. I had done nothing wrong. Occasionally, the door would open, and someone would look down at me then close the door. It must have been the weekend because I wasn't going to school. I thought maybe I would be off the steps soon.

The morning turned into the afternoon. I could hear muffled sounds of laughter and every so often a knock on the basement door. Once again, I had to go to the bathroom, and once again, my pleas were not answered. My bottom was completely numb, and the constant rocking back and forth did little to help my bladder. When the door finally opened, I was handed a peanut butter sandwich. I begged to go to the bathroom, but there was no response from Janet as she shut the door.

The light in the basement stairs began to dim. I could not bear the pain in my kidneys or the loss of feeling in my legs. I wanted to stand for a moment, but I was afraid of what might happen if the door opened. I focused on eating the sandwich. The edges of the bread were hard, and it tasted funny, but I dared not cross the woman by not eating it. I was certain that there would be consequences if I didn't, and I would discover later that I was right.

As the afternoon turned into evening, I began to lose sight of my surroundings. Eventually, all I could see was the reflection of my shadow that was created by a small opening at the bottom of the door. I could still hear voices and laughter from just beyond the stairwell. Were they laughing at me?

The door finally opened, and I was told to stand. I grabbed the banister and pulled myself up, but I was unable to stand and fell back onto the step. "Get up!"

The sound of her voice was horrifying. My entire being was in shock. I needed to stand, and I needed to do it now! I grabbed the banister and stood, holding onto it with everything I had in me. I could not move because there was no feeling in my legs, and my sides were in immense pain. I dared not pee myself. My eyes were trying to adjust to the light again as I attempted to look at her face.

I could feel Janet staring at me, waiting for me to move. She enjoyed every minute of it. She was in control. I was a puppet, and she was tugging on all the strings, manipulating my every move with her voice. My pain was her pleasure. She was able to control me without retaliation; she was now my master, and I was her slave.

As I regained my sight, I was finally able to look at her face. It was the face I would never become accustomed to, the face of a woman without compassion, who bore a signature gap between her front teeth. It was a face that I would fear for a long time, a face that I would attempt not to look at, and a face I would dream about in my bed at night.

I do not recall how I made it to the bathroom. I was determined not to get off the toilet until I went, no matter what the consequences. I could smell the strong scent of urine as my bladder finally opened. I tried pushing, but this only made the pain in my side worse. The woman stood above me in silence, listening to the sounds as I sat there. My head was lowered to my knees, and I hoped that I would be allowed to finish. I wondered where my brother was and prayed he would somehow protect me. But I didn't see or hear his voice the entire day.

The sound of urine flowing finally stopped, and I slid off the toilet. My sides were still hurting, and it was difficult for me to pull my underwear up. I kept my head down for fear of getting hit. "Go to bed," she said.

As she opened the door to the stairs leading to my bunk bed, I discovered why I hadn't seen my brother. He was suffering the same fate that I was. There he was, sitting on the stairs with his head down. He was silent, motionless, and didn't look at me as I passed. I wanted to grab hold of him and run. But I had to keep moving up the stairs and into my bed. The door closed, and there we were in darkness. My brother was sitting on the steps, in silence. I could barely see the top of his head through the spindles lining the stairwell while I was lying in the top bunk. I whispered quietly to him, but there was no response. Did this woman have control over my brother too? I tried to stay awake long enough to see that my brother made it to bed, but I was exhausted and fell asleep.

The following days were very confusing. We were sent off to school wearing hand-me-down clothes and shoes that didn't fit right. I know it sounds like there was nothing positive given to us in this house. Why can't I type anything positive? I am not going to say that good things didn't happen, because eventually there would be some good that came about, but not for a very long time. I will talk a bit about school later.

After school, it was pretty much the same routine. I figured out that Janet was keeping us separated to gain control of us individually. Had my brother been next to me, the outcome might have been different.

The stairs were a constant challenge to my mind as well as my body. Sitting there, I would wonder about my real parents. I tried to remember what they looked like. Though I would get glimpses of them in my dreams, I couldn't form their faces in my mind anymore. Even so, I never gave up on them. I truly thought that I would eventually see them and find my way home.

I learned to block out the sounds coming from the house above me. The only sound that mattered was the opening of the door. I was frightened of it as well as thankful. However, the stairs were not my enemy. It was the person that sent me there. I actually welcomed the stairs because I knew I would be safe if I sat quietly. I can still see them today. I can see my spot and feel the wood beneath me; touch the banister and run my hand across it. I can smell the scent coming from the crawl spaces on either side of me and see the items on the shelving above and the color gray surrounding me. The stairs will always have a place in my vault, both a protective sanctuary and a nightmare that cannot be separated.

I would only see my brother when we were allowed to eat. We sat at a foldup table and folding chairs separated from the rest of the family. We were set up in the corner of the kitchen while the rest of the family ate in the dining area. There was plenty of room for "family" at the dining table. When we were finished eating, we would return the table and chairs to the basement.

Our food was not always what the rest of the family ate. I learned how to make Carnation Instant milk and how to mix peanut butter and jelly together to form a gooey concoction. I learned how to tell the difference between their bread and ours. Our cereal was in a bag instead of a box. We were banned from the treats overflowing in the cubbies. The treasure trove of Hostess Ho-Ho's cream-filled Twinkies, cupcakes, and the family- favorite pink marshmallow-domed cupcakes that were locked away in the basement freezer were not to be shared with us.

I could sense that my brother was quickly gaining courage. I could see it in his eyes when he looked at me. We weren't allowed to talk, but I had seen that look before and it gave me hope. When we were separated again, I kept his eyes in my thoughts.

My days on the stairs slowly dwindled as I became much more useful doing chores around the house. I was a willing participant because of the tremendous fear I had of Janet. Cleaning also allowed me to move and keep my mind busy. One of my tasks was to scrub the kitchen floor. It was a white ceramic tile floor that consisted of one-inch by one-inch squares. I would start at the entrance to the house, working my little hands in a circular motion, making sure I got into all the crevices.

I could tell that Janet was surprised that I was conforming to her demands so easily. What choice did I have? At least I could go to the bathroom, and that was a victory for me. While I worked, I was always on the lookout for my brother. He was somewhere else in the house, out of sight, but we were connected; I could feel it.

I had very little contact with the three other children in the beginning. I was about four years older than the youngest. The middle boy was about the same age as my brother, and the oldest was in his early teens. They didn't participate in the many chores that I was taught to do. They could also eat the chocolate-filled pies from the basement treasure box and pull treats from the cubbies without asking. They played with friends and watched TV, stayed up late at night, and were shown much love and compassion. It didn't take long for me to figure out that these three kids were not foster kids; they belonged to Janet and her husband.

My brother and I had no playtime. We were either sitting on the steps, standing in a corner, or doing chores. Janet had full control over me, and she knew what to do if I didn't acquiesce to her demands. She was able to make me do anything. Daniel was not as easily pushed into doing chores. Most of the time, he sat idle in defiance. He was beginning to get his strength back and preparing to fight some battles. He started saying "no" within a few short weeks after we arrived at this whatever you want to call it—certainly not home! I would catch him smiling at me occasionally, to show me that he was okay; I admired him so.

My battles were different. I didn't have the confidence my brother did. Janet scared me to death. I was taught all kinds of things: how to properly clean the carpet, dust mop the hardwood floors, dust the furniture, and scrub the many types of flooring. How to iron clothing, fold laundry, and sweep the stairs. How to properly clean the surface of the kitchen cupboards, how to put away the groceries and fold the brown paper bags, and how to brew coffee and pack my foster father's lunch. How to rake leaves, pull weeds, and mow the lawn. I also learned how to properly make the beds—everyone's beds!

There are some basic rules when cleaning. For example, does it make sense to clean the carpet before or after you dust? Well, in this house, if you dusted and then cleaned the carpet, you would have to dust again. If you dust mopped before you cleaned the carpet, you would have to dust mop again. You always had to clean the carpet first, using a red push broom. It had little brush rollers that would empty the dirt into a tray that I would open and clean each time I used it. Trust me when I say I cleaned it. You never knew when there was going to be an inspection.

Dusting was an art of its own. It was important to use a clean dusting cloth and Pledge (lemon fresh was my brand). When you dusted the wooden chairs, you made sure that you dusted from the top down. It was critical to get in between each rung of the chair and the cross-supports at the base. When dusting the wooden tabletops, you had to lift off every item, dust the tabletop and the legs all the way to the floor, and then place dusted items back in the proper location. Proper location was very important. Improper item placement had consequences.

Dust mopping the hardwood floor had to be done right too. First you swept the hardwood floor with a broom and picked up any loose dirt with the dust pan. No, I'm sorry—first you moved any furniture that was on the hardwood floor onto the area rug and *then* you did the above. You sprayed a bit of Pledge on the dust mop. Starting by lifting the edge of the area rug, you placed the dust mop under it, and went around the entire perimeter of the rug. Then you went in a sweeping motion starting in one corner and ending up back in the same corner. Remember now, this had to be done right!

The kitchen cupboards required ammonia and warm water first. This was followed by a thorough rubdown with Murphy's oil soap which was then polished off so you could see a beautiful glow. And by the way, all the wood paneling in this house required the same cleaning process; there was a lot of it!

I think you understand where I am going with this. I did not acquire these skills overnight. Nor did my ability to clean and do a good job come without a heavy price. I would spend many hours (sometimes the entire day) doing and redoing the same piece of furniture. I would scrub the same floor over and over again. The cupboards and wood paneling, if they were alive, would have begged me to stop touching them. A glass mirror would laugh at me, and the bedsheets would become angry because of my relentless pursuit to make the bed perfectly.

My role in this house eventually became obvious. I was, in every sense of the word, a true housemaid. When I wasn't doing chores, I was standing in the corner or sitting on the stairs. I would much rather be doing the chores. I was beginning to be quite good at it. Chores gave me purpose, though not in the normal sense of the word. It was something that I could cling to that made me feel a little bit normal. I took pride in my work even though I was never given credit for what I did.

I need to stop a moment. I want to make it undeniably clear that what I am putting down on paper is very real. I do not pretend to be a writer. This journey is based upon what is still crisp and clear in my head after many years of silence. One of my obsessive compulsions that can be attributed to this childhood experience is my need to try and do things in perfect sequence. Unfortunately, for me this is not possible. I know what happened, and it is in the vault, but I cannot put one page in front of the other without mixing the pages up at times. The outcome is the same; the experience is the same, but I may have done the cupboards before I did the floors. I may have been a year younger or a year older. It may have happened in December instead of January or the day before instead of the day after. This doesn't really matter. What matters is what happened, happened.

Back to the vault. I would eventually be familiar with every nook and cranny in the house, know what every drawer and cupboard held, and be aware of what order things were to be kept. The canned peas were to be stacked neatly next to the corn. The bread was not to be in danger of being crushed. The milk belonged on the bottom shelf and to the right, not to be confused with the fake Carnation instant milk on the left. The brown paper bags were to be neatly folded and tucked away. The separation of items that belonged to us and what belonged to the real family was quite clear. It was my duty to put the groceries in their proper place.

The laundry was not at all a fun chore for me, but after-school hours and weekend hours had to be filled somehow. Janet taught me how to iron clothing in the basement. I would be set up with an iron and ironing board, accompanied by a big pile of clothing in a laundry basket. I would spend many days after school ironing. The strange thing, other than the fact that most of what I was ironing was my foster father's underwear and white T-shirts, was that I had to do this task *in my underwear*. I wasn't allowed to wear clothes while doing this. This was yet another control tactic that this woman carefully planned to lower my self-esteem.

Janet was always watching, keeping me in check. There was a basement window that was next to the entryway of the house. I was constantly in fear of someone catching me standing in my underwear, ironing underwear. I would stand in one spot for hours ironing and then re-ironing the same clothes late into the evening. I had better fold them the way she taught me; there was only one way that was acceptable. There had to be creases in the items that were ironed. They were to be in the precise locations, or they went back in the laundry basket.

I became very good at ironing and folding clothes. I would put every piece of clothing in the proper location. Like the groceries, everything had its place, and it had better be in the correct spot. I learned quickly that if the clothes were not where they belonged, they would be tossed back into a basket for me to refold and put away. Laundry would become one of the top three priorities on my task list in this home. Unlike most of the other chores, I hated doing laundry.

Let's spend a little time at school now. I loved going to school. As soon as I stepped onto the school bus, I became a different person. I wasn't bound by the chains that held me in place at home. Free to speak to others and able to sit where I wanted to sit, I would morph into a child that wasn't afraid. I needed to be seen as someone who was normal. Wanting to be recognized and respected, I began to build a reputation as a tough guy. To that end, I would fight in class and challenge kids in the gym. I wanted to be liked and noticed. The awkward clothes that I was wearing no longer bothered me. I found friendship and respect with my schoolmates, including those I fought with.

As I grew older, I would become close to three schoolmates that understood the person that I really was. I was not the tough guy that everyone thought I was. I would rather protect than fight. I looked out for others being picked on.

I was weak, however, in so many ways. I was afraid to challenge anyone at home. This was not the case with my brother. He was willing to sacrifice his body and resisted most anything that he was told to do. He found pleasure in upsetting the basement freezer, which was essentially a frozen treasure box. He sat in my spot on the stairs literally for weeks before he finally revealed where he hid the goods. They were right above his head, tucked behind some rags on the stairwell.

He paid another price for messing with the freezer in the basement. The foster father took him to the basement and whipped him with a belt. This did not faze my brother in the least. He took the beating with pride, no crying or sounds coming from his mouth. Daniel never lost his strength to defy pain or authority. In his world, he was the winner; he was the strong one. The person striking him had no meaning or purpose, and the outcome didn't matter.

He still smiled at me a lot when he was being punished. He knew that it helped me cope; even though I was broken, he would be strong. It was kind of ironic; I was the tough guy at school, but I couldn't even fathom doing what Daniel did at home. I was the coward; humbled and humiliated, in control of nothing.

As time continued to tick away, I experienced just a bit of interaction with the three boys. I was drawn to the love and affection they received, wanting to taste what I once had. The separation of food and clothing, playtime and normalcy, regimented chores and punishment kept my brother and me from getting that taste. The brothers enjoyed basking in attention and did nothing to help us. We would often get blamed and punished for things that they did. I will share some of these things later.

Janet had a younger sister who would show up at the house a lot. She did not look at all like her sister. She was very pretty, lived in high heels and miniskirts, and drove a fancy car. Unfortunately for us, she was also a lot like Janet. She would tease me by grabbing me from the back and trying to pull my pants down to expose my private parts. I hated her for doing that. I was very self-conscious of my small frame, and these people knew it. Laughter and humiliation at the expense of a child—how can that make an adult feel good inside, please tell me?

MY REBECCA

One day after school, I was introduced to another foster child. She was a cute little girl with long reddish-brown hair. "Her name is Rebecca. She is your sister," I was told. What? I had a sister? Was she my real sister? Yes, she was! I had no idea that I had a younger sister. She was three and a half years younger than me and must have been born after we were placed in foster care. My brother never mentioned it because he probably didn't know either. We were pulled from our home and placed into this crazy system together.

The nightmare began for her as it had for me. She was placed on the chair. Janet used a razor blade to cut off Rebecca's long beautiful hair. I only have two pictures of my childhood in my possession. One is of me when I was living in my world of Rudy. I was cute and had a beautiful head of blond hair. The other one is a picture of my sister Rebecca with her hair chopped off. Her beauty was taken away from her. She looked like an ugly boy.

I cried for her; I wanted to help her. She was my blood, my real sister. She was someone who belonged to my family, not theirs. I wanted to get to know her, to love her, and to protect her. I failed miserably, and I live my life knowing that I let my sister endure terrible suffering and I didn't stop it. It haunts me so. I know in my heart that many of the scars embedded in her belong to me too. I contributed to her suffering because I was a coward.

Janet was cunning. She knew how to keep my brother separated from my sister so he did not witness many of the cruel acts that were forced upon her. I was not spared this because Janet knew that I was afraid and would not stop her. She knew that she would instill more fear in me by watching my sister suffer. She knew that I would not tell my brother because of it, and I didn't.

Remember when I mentioned the pages in the vault? One of the other problems is that the bad things that happened get squeezed together. Time has no boundaries. The weeks or the months or the years living in this place do not make sense. When I think about my sister, all I see is suffering. How can I offer something that was good if I do not have it? With my sister there is nothing good, not a single page.

"You will eat this!" I can visualize the kitchen and the eat-in kitchen area as though I am standing in it today. Like many other locations in the house, the kitchen possessed evil. It was like living in the twilight zone.

My sister sat in a chair with her hands tied behind her back, wearing a cloth diaper for a bib. Janet forced food into her mouth with a large metal spoon. Rebecca's cheeks were stretched to the limits. "Swallow the food! Did you swallow?"

I could hear my sister's voice. "Yes." It was a high-pitched muffled sound that was difficult to hear because of all the food that was in the way. It was a sound that begged not to be slapped and to be allowed to swallow. Her cheeks were on fire from the repeated blows to her face. The endless questioning was followed by a slap to the face. It didn't matter if the answer was a yes or no.

I was in the background facing Rebecca in the twilight zone. I saw the look in her eyes. She was staring at Janet with such immense fear that it would not allow me to look away. I wanted it to stop. I wanted to help her, but I didn't. I was in fear for myself. What would happen if I tried to stop it? Would this woman make it even worse for my sister? Would I get the belt or suffer the same fate as she did?

The food that my sister refused to eat or could not eat was put back into the refrigerator for the next meal. This would go on for days. She would be tied up with a bib around her neck and the same scene would play out until the last bit of the disgusting food was gone. This would happen many times throughout Rebecca's stay in this home. Each time I would be forced to witness it, and each time I did nothing. I am sorry. I must stop again for a bit.

The foster father figure was like the one in our second home. He would come home from work, go to his favorite room, and sit back in his recliner. At times he would visit his hobby shop and work on remote-control airplanes. He did not participate in much of what was going on, but he was just as guilty for allowing it to happen. I often wondered how he could just sit back and not feel something for us. Maybe Janet had control over him too. When he gave us the belt, it was because of his wife demanding it.

My sister's suffering tormented me. I didn't have to worry about my brother, but Rebecca was helpless. I felt like I should do something or say something to someone, maybe at school or when my caseworker showed up. But I kept silent. I struggled with the consequences of my silence and surrendering to my fears.

The haunting memory on this next page is stuck to the one above and cannot be separated. I need to share the layout of the house so you can understand what I am about to tell you. As you entered the house, you stepped into the eat-in kitchen area. Next to this was the kitchen. As I mentioned before, the basement stairs' entrance was off the kitchen. From the kitchen, you moved into the living room space that had sliding glass doors opening to a front porch with railings and a covered aluminum roof. As you left the living room, you walked up three steps to the next level. To the right was the bedroom slash foster father's lair. In the center was another bedroom, and to the left was the bathroom. The entrance to the third level of the house was opposite the center bedroom's hallway door.

The day it happened, it was midafternoon, and I was involved in one of my daily chores. Janet was hosting company in the living room. I had no idea who these people were nor did I care. As I entered the center bedroom on the second level, I heard a muffled voice. It sounded like someone was trying to speak while being smothered by a pillowcase, and it was coming from behind the open bedroom door.

As I peered behind the door, I was horrified by what I saw. It was my sister. She was wearing a one-piece conductor's suit. It was light blue with dark blue lines running perpendicular to the floor. It had a long zipper that started at the waist and ended up at the top of the neckline. The suit was put on Rebecca backwards so she would not be able to unzip it. The sleeves of the suit were brought behind her and tied together in the middle of her back. Her arms and hands were bound tight. She was wearing a homemade straitjacket.

When I looked at her face, I couldn't believe my eyes. She had a rag tied around the center of her mouth with a sock stuffed inside it. She was rocking back and forth, lifting one leg, then the other and leaning forward. She looked at me, trying to speak. I can see her face now and again, and it haunts me. It will always haunt me. It haunts me with the other dark secrets, but I have a difficult time dealing with what happened to her.

I was brave enough to pull back the rag and pull out the sock to try and understand what she was saying. "I have to go to the bathroom." Not only was she bound and gagged, but she was suffering one of Janet's favorite control tactics shared by me and my brother. I knew how it felt. Experience also taught me that standing to try and hold it in was much more difficult than sitting.

I gently put the sock back in her mouth and pulled the rag back into place. I had better get moving before I get caught. I felt sick inside as I put the door back into position, hiding Rebecca from sight.

I could not keep myself away. I wanted so desperately to help her. The visitors in the living room gave me an opportunity to check on her. She again looked into my eyes, and I could barely make out her muffled voice saying, "I have to go." She was broken. She could not hold it any longer. She stopped the rocking motion and the lifting of her legs. As she leaned forward, I could hear the sound of urine splashing against her clothing. It rushed out of her as though a hose had just burst. The smell of strong urine flowed endlessly down her captive clothing and onto the floor. I thought it would never stop.

Janet had won: she wanted this to happen. She wanted my sister to break. My brother and I never lost this painful battle, but to do this to a little girl could only be described as pure evil.

She stood bound and gagged in that puddle of urine for hours while this woman played host to her guests. Why didn't I do something? I could have pulled my sister from behind the door and exposed her to the guests. I could have called the police and told them to peer into the back window because they would not have believed me. I could have removed her from the homemade straitjacket, pulled the gag from her mouth, walked her to the bathroom, and dealt the consequences. I did nothing.

When it was finally discovered and her face was forced to the floor and rubbed in it, I cried and wanted to die. Yes, I was forced to witness this. She was treated like an animal, and still I did nothing to stop it. I was paralyzed with fear. May God forgive me.

If you are wondering where my brother was at the time, I cannot tell you. If you are wondering where the three boys were, I cannot tell you. I remember the guests and my freedom to witness the fate of my sister. It was like Janet planned for me to be made part of it. She enjoyed the control she had over me, over us. Witnessing these terrible acts would only make me weaker, and she knew it.

It is difficult for me to remove myself from these thoughts when I peer into the vault. It feels like I am there, living in the past. I can see things, touch things, smell the air, hear the voices, and see their faces. I can relive the scene as if it happened yesterday. Why do I continue to allow myself to go back? I have lived with these secrets for five decades.

Why do I go back? Maybe it is because of the dreams. Maybe it is because of Rebecca. Maybe it is because I have such tremendous guilt. Maybe it is because I want to forgive and be forgiven. Maybe it is because I want to help others and spare them from a similar fate. Maybe it is because of that special connection with the person that is hanging on the wall in every room of my house today. Yes, these things make it worth it.

It was another late afternoon, and I was sitting in my spot on the basement stairs. I must have done something wrong. One of the items on the shelves above me was a box of mothballs. It was one of those days when I was feeling pity for myself. I thought about the life I was living and saw no hope. I thought about my daily routine and the insignificance of my role in this family. I thought about my sister and my cowardliness. Reaching up, I grabbed the box, opened it up, and popped two mothballs into my mouth. I swallowed them whole. *This will take care of it. This will end it.*

I sat there waiting for something to happen. I started to think maybe this wasn't such a good idea. I started to panic, wondering if I was going to die. I wanted to live! I didn't want to leave my brother and sister! After a while, I began to feel sick and started to heave. I stuck my head into the crawl space and vomited.

I think many people at a certain point in their lives think about committing suicide, right? Am I trying to justify my actions? Probably. Thank God it was only a couple of mothballs.

Before we move on to the cabin in the woods, I feel the need to type something that might lift the spirits of my fellow readers and make you smile. I bet many of you have fond memories of playing these games.

School gave me the freedom to escape from whatever you want to call it at home. My schoolmates and I used to play hockey in the back of the classroom with a tightly bound round piece of paper. We had a lot of fun playing this game. The brush burns we got from the floor never stopped us from trying to land a goal.

Some of my favorite games involved money. We would toss a coin and try to get it as close to the wall as possible. The person whose coin was closest would gather up his winnings. We would do this in the back of the classroom or in the boys' bathroom. One day, I would be king, and on others I would borrow from my friends just so I could play. It was just pennies, nickels, and on rare occasions a quarter. The money really wasn't important; it was the competition that made it so much fun.

Another coin game that I loved was played on a flat surface. The person had three attempts to flick the coin across the surface (usually one of our school desks) to get it as close to the edge without falling off. The person with the most skill would be able to have the coin teeter on the edge without falling off.

In another game, the person had three pennies. You had to flick one penny between the other two and land it inside the finger goalie of the other person on the opposite end. If at any time the coin didn't pass completely through the other two coins, you would lose your turn. I liked this one a lot!

Okay, one more. Super balls! My friends would bring in all sizes and shapes. My favorite super balls were the ones that looked like pool balls. Our secluded spot to slam these little power-packed spheres to the walls, ceilings, and floors (and sometimes ourselves) was in the boys' bathroom. The teachers would confiscate some of them if we were caught, but that never stopped us. My friends had an endless supply.

Do any of those games ring a bell? I just needed to think of something good before we begin our journey to the cabin in the woods. I hope you are still with me!

THE CABIN IN THE WOODS

The family had a cabin located in the woods far from home, in a secluded area. We would visit the cabin over summer break, spending weeks at a time there. I hated the ritual of packing and loading the Volkswagen van. I hated the trip out because my brother, sister, and I had to sit on the floorboards or packed in the back with the items that we were taking. I hated it because we would drive through a town and pass by a school, a dairy farm, and most importantly, my sanctuary. Yes, we drove past Mom and Rudy. How crazy was that! Most of all, I hated it because of what happened in the woods.

The chores inside the cabin were like the chores I would do at home. I would focus on doing a good job to please Janet. When I was in this mode, I did not pay attention to the surroundings or what my brother or sister were doing. Always on the defensive, striving to stay unnoticed, I would try to stretch the chores out so time would pass in my favor. When I was told to do something, I would do it without question. I wanted to do well. I needed to do well. It was the only thing that made me feel somewhat normal.

When the mindless chores were finished, my brother and I were given rakes and told to rake the woods. We would rake the woods until it got dark. We did this day after day after day. Try to imagine raking the woods. We were told to start at the top of the hill and rake in a straight line and were warned not to talk to each other. My brother didn't fight this task because I was with him. It was very rare that we were together. We would talk to each other with our heads down while raking next to each other. There was the random surprise inspection to make sure we were making progress, but at least we were able to spend time together. It was hard work. I was glad that my brother didn't fight this one though. Rebecca would be sitting or standing somewhere else. Usually standing.

When we weren't raking, we would gather up branches and twigs for outdoor fires. We were instructed to place them in huge piles on the outer edges of the woods. This chore didn't bother me as much. We didn't have to move in a straight line, and it was more difficult for the family to keep an eye on us. The woods were filled with many creatures. We enjoyed the brief encounters that we had with them. There were snakes and salamanders, squirrels, chipmunks, centipedes, millipedes, and flying bugs of all different kinds. There were beautiful birds and the occasional annoying sound of the blue jays. Aside from the physical labor, the battles with horseflies and mosquitoes were the biggest problem. The horsefly bites hurt! Oh, and there was the skunk cabbage. Today when I smell the odor of a dead skunk in the road, I am immediately drawn back to this place.

The rain was no longer my friend because it meant staying indoors. Staying indoors meant sitting or standing for hours.

Strange and terrible things happened in the woods. After one arrival and unpacking of the Volkswagen, it was discovered that a cake that was brought had been partially squished. The three of us had to figure out which one of us did it. For some reason on this day, we all stood firm in denial; after all, we were not guilty. Maybe it was because we knew what the outcome was going to be. The three of us sat down to a meal consisting of one squished cake. We couldn't leave the table until every crumb was gone.

There was a lake close by that had a small beach that only members of the community could use. A lifeguard would always be close by, monitoring the roped-off area that we could swim in. I hated going to this place with a passion. The three boys could do whatever they wanted. They could build castles in the sand, bask in the sun, jump off the docks and swim or run in and out of the water. We did not have these opportunities. We were told to get in the water and stay in it. The water was always cold and murky. We would walk aimlessly around in the shallow water trying to stay warm. The only good thing about this was that we could pee while being undetected.

The middle boy would sometimes take me onto the dock and throw me off into the deep end. I could not swim. When my head went below the water, I could not see anything in front of me, and the gurgling sounds in my ears made me disoriented. The water was dark. There was a lot of seaweed (that's what I call it) everywhere, especially outside the roped-off area. I would surface, trying to catch my breath, and paddle frantically like a dog to try and reach the ropes. The boy thought it was funny. You would think others on the beach would say something, but they never did.

When the "playtime adventure" was over, we would gather up the shovels, sand pails, and blow-up beach balls that the youngest boy played with. We would shake out the beach blankets and fold them neatly. The Volkswagen van would be loaded, and we would head back to the cabin. I was so glad to be out of the water.

When we arrived at the cabin, my job was to unload the van and bring everything to the table outside the cabin. The beach towels needed to be air-dried, and the toys had their own place to be inventoried and stored. I could not find one of the sand pails and its shovel. Panic set in. I searched frantically for them.

On this particular outing, Janet's sister and daughter were out for the weekend. Her sister would take over on this one. I said that I couldn't find them. "Find them! I don't care how long it takes. Just bring them here." I looked everywhere. They were not in the van or anywhere on the pathway from the van to the cabin. In my mind, I knew that I had to find them. If I didn't, I would be searching until the sun went down and back on the hunt the next morning.

I was a clever child and began to think logically after the initial fear settled a bit. If they were not in the van or somewhere on the pathway, they must still be at the beach. Maybe they fell out of the van while driving back to the cabin. There was only one choice.

Stay and live with what I knew was going to happen, or run like the dickens down the road and back to the beach. I decided to run!

I ran as though a bear was chasing me. As I was running, I looked in the road and on either side in the ditches. There were twists and turns in the road, and as I rounded the third, there they were! My logic paid off, and I would be safe.

I picked up the pail and shovel and ran back to the cabin. It seemed as though very little time had passed while I was gone. I guess I was wrong. As soon as I approached the table, I heard her screaming. "Where were you? Why didn't you answer me?" I held up the sand pail and shovel and said that they had fallen out of the van and onto the road. I had to run back and get them.

In a normal situation, you would think that I would be praised. Not so. She pulled me to the side of the cabin, picked up something hard, and began hitting me with it. She hit my bottom, lower back, the arm that I was defending myself with, and the tops of my legs. She hit me forever …

I guess it must be allowed to have someone not designated as your guardian beat a child. She wasn't my foster mother or foster father. I had no feeling when it was over. It was not like the numbness I felt on the stairs. I was sitting on a cushion of broken blood vessels. Whenever my body recovered from the numbness of the stairs, it was okay. But as I began to get feeling back from the beating, all I can remember was the warmth fading away and pain taking its place. I wanted to stand because it hurt so badly. I wanted to feel the numbness that I was accustomed to when sitting for hours. The ride back home was challenging, to say the least. The only comfort I had was the thought of leaving the cabin in the woods behind us for another season. It took a long time to heal.

Back home the Sunday before school, my brother and I were getting ready for our usual bath that we had to take together. When my clothing was removed, my entire backside was completely black and blue. I could only see the tops of my legs and some of my butt. My arm and lower back were also bruised. It scared me to death. Janet went and got her sister and brought her into the bathroom. They both started laughing! Why would someone laugh at something like that? Why wouldn't there be an "Oh my God, what did I do?" or "I am so sorry. I can't believe I did this."

I was beaten and bruised, and now, humiliated. We were not loved by these people. We were simply objects that could be manipulated and toyed with. Our suffering brought them pleasure. My brother did not shed tears often, but this incident was traumatic for him. He loved me.

The next day at school, I wanted to tell someone. I wanted to show someone and make these people pay so I would be moved to another foster home to be free from this nightmare. But I stayed silent. Once again, I surrendered to my fears. I sat in the wooden classroom seats and absorbed the pain while trying to act normal. I would hide the bruises when changing for gym by being late or make some excuse for not having my gym gear. At this young age I was (and still am) very good at hiding both the inner emotional scars and the physical scars.

My brother never forgot that moment. He placed it somewhere in his head along with the others. He was going to get us out of that home somehow.

I am going to jump ahead in time for just a moment. This relates to the cabin in the woods. I was married, and my wife and I were thinking about becoming foster parents. I told the person that came to our house that I wanted to help children because I, too, had been in foster care. I told her how important it was for us to help children feel loved and comforted when their world is falling apart in front of their eyes. I did not want any child to feel what I felt growing up in foster care. No one deserves to be taken away from the only thing they know and feel helpless and abandoned. No one should be taken away and then taken advantage of. When she asked me what was the last foster home I was in, I said "the Peters." The first thing that came from her mouth was "You know a child died in that family?" Supposedly, the child, while spending time out at the cabin, fell off the toilet and died.

I cannot tell you the anger that welled up inside me. I lived in that home. I know what went on. The welfare system knew that a little child had died while in the care of these people. I cannot say that poor child was abused. I cannot say that child didn't fall off the toilet and die in an unfortunate accident. That may have been the case. What I do know is what happened to us while were there. I think about that child and wonder what happened to him. How did he die? When he fell off the toilet, did he hit his head? Did he have some sort of physical defect such as a weak heart? Was he sick at the time? I pray it was one of these things. There must have been an investigation, so foul play must have been ruled out. But it still bothers me. A little boy lost his life. Why would this person bring this up so many years later?

I never became a foster parent. God blessed us instead with a special child. Our time would be devoted to raising a child with autism. That is another story. I thank God every day for that blessing. My son keeps me strong and focused. My boy and I are filled with unconditional love that no one can ever take away.

COLD

We all know what Christmas is about. It is the story of baby Jesus being born, going to church on Christmas eve, Christmas lights and decorations, good food and family gatherings, but most of all for a child, presents. What could possibly be bad about this day? The tree was decorated with the family ornaments, garlands, and the old-fashioned candelabra bulbs topped with a lighted star. I should know; I decorated it! There were presents under the tree and stockings stuffed to the brim with candy. Who wouldn't feel good waking up to that?

We were told to sit on one of the three steps. There, we watched as the presents were handed out and opened in front of us. As the pile grew smaller, a normal reaction would be to cling to the possibility that one or two of them might belong to one of us. I finally received a gift or two. It was just clothing, but at least it was something. My brother and sister got nothing. When all the gifts were finally opened, it was time to pass out the stockings. Janet stood up and went into the kitchen area. When she returned, she had two stockings that were packed with something. I can hear those words now. "Boys and girls that are bad get coal, rotten potatoes, and oranges." My brother and sister were each handed a stocking. The contents were exactly as she said: rotten oranges, potatoes with long, scary dangling eyes, and real black coal.

Can you imagine what it must have felt like sitting there holding that stocking while everyone looked at you? The first thing that came to my mind was *will she make them eat this*? Thank God that didn't happen. By the way, the next Christmas played out the same.

Why I was spared? Because I conformed. I allowed things to happen to me and didn't fight. My brother and sister were not bad little children. Who would want to eat food that was disgusting? Being bound and gagged and forced to pee yourself made you a bad little girl? My brother's defiance was justified. He was not a bad little boy. He was strong and fought for all the right reasons.

Winter was another one of our enemies. We would be told to go outside in the cold, and we were not allowed to come back in until Janet decided to let us in. Rebecca would be wearing rubber boots with no socks on. She did have socks on her hands. This was bad enough. What happens when you are out in the cold for a bit? You tend to have to go to the bathroom. Rebecca would walk aimlessly back and forth while leaning forward and pushing her thighs together. She would beg to be let in. Sometimes, she could hold it and sometimes not. She didn't give up easily. She would fight to hold it for as long as possible, hoping that she could be able to go like a normal human being. Why didn't the neighbors do something? And as for me …

It was very unusual to find just my sister and I alone together. I remember once we were sitting shivering away in our usual spot on the floorboards in the Volkswagen van. We were in a shopping mall so Janet must have had to take us with her. It was very dark, and we could barely see each other. Rebecca was about seven years old at the time. She reached out and took my hand. I thought that she wanted comfort, and it made me feel good inside. This was not case. She tried to put my hand down the front of her, and I immediately pulled away. This was not normal. It only happened once, and I never asked her why she did it. Was she just trying to be funny? We both sat shivering in the dark without saying a word. I hate the cold now; it makes me feel vulnerable. How ridiculous, right?

I feel that sharing my dreams as they happened helps me, because they are a result of what is in the vault. Dreams can either torment or help a person cope with trauma. I hope this makes sense to you as well. Not all my dreams are bad. Some, like this one I'll share now, comfort me to this day.

I was lying in my bed on the third level, in a deep sleep. Clouds were forming all around me, and

I felt like I was floating in the air along with them. Suddenly, a man started walking toward me. He was wearing a beautiful flowing blue and white robe. He put his arms around me and held me close. I could not see his face, but I felt peace. I felt safe and comforted, but most of all, *I felt loved.* I never wanted to let go.

When I awoke, I could feel something leaving my body. I had very little religious background at the time other than my wonderful stay in Summersville. Jesus was with me that night. I know it. He was always with me, and he is with me right now.

I often wondered about my parents while lying in bed at night. I had fleeting dreams, but they made little sense. I would, however, finally get to meet them after a very long time.

MOM? DAD?

One day, while sitting in our special kitchen area eating our tasteless cereal bathed in the "shaken but not stirred" powdered milk, we were told that we were going to see our mother and father. I didn't believe Janet at first, but it happened. We were dressed in clothes that I had never seen before. I had shoes that fit. I was so excited I could hardly contain myself. I am pretty sure it was a caseworker that picked us up, but she wasn't the one I was familiar with.

We were taken downtown to a large building and rode the elevator to one of the upper floors. The caseworker sat us down on some chairs that were lined up in the hallway. We sat waiting for a long time before we were taken into a room. As we entered, my brother and sister ran to my dad and he welcomed them with open arms. I wanted Mom! But I did not recognize my mother. She looked so different from what I remembered, and she was acting very strange. I thought I was going to see a beautiful woman with long black hair and a beautiful smile, wearing a dress like I had imagined in my dreams. A woman that couldn't wait to pick me up and hold me tight; a woman longing to hold her son. What I did see frightened me. She kept pulling her front teeth out and showing them to me. Her voice was very deep, and mixed with her Southern drawl, it sounded scary.

Her first words, "Hi, Mikey" immediately lit up the neurons to my past. I remembered "Mikey" and that comforted me some, but she was still showing me her teeth. I tried to get closer to her, but I didn't know what to say so I tried, "Hi, Mom. I missed you so much!" That didn't change her expression; it was like she was so focused on her inner thoughts that she couldn't connect to her own son. She didn't hug me or pick me up. I was so lost. I didn't know how to act.

I stayed with Mom for the entire meeting. I would glance over at Dad; he looked just the way I remembered him. His hair was still jet-black, and his Southern accent hadn't changed either. I wanted to get close to him to see if he still had that smell, but he was so engaged with my brother and sister and I was desperately trying to get the mom-son connection I longed for in my dreams.

"Mom, do you remember our bath and the bubbles? Mom, can you sing our song" I love that song. Mom, please sing me our song …"

I got nothing. I didn't understand; the memories and the dreams stored in my mind started to crumble. She was not in my world that day; she was somewhere else. I started to wonder if I would ever be going home.

I felt like we were being watched. There were glass windows all around us, and the caseworker was always in sight. I didn't feel what I thought I was going to feel. I was lost. I was confused. It was as though I was meeting my mother for the very first time. My father was talking to my brother and sister huddled in a corner. The look in his eyes as they traded conversation resembled that of a boy receiving a gift. The opportunity to tell him what was going on in our foster home took hold.

When the meeting was over, we were shuffled back to a different room and sat down to wait for the caseworker. As she entered the room, she stopped and motioned me to come with her, down the hallway into yet another room. She sat me down and started to tell me what my brother and sister had shared with my father.

"I am going to ask you some questions. Please do not be afraid to answer. You are safe with me. Okay?"

"Okay, but what is wrong with my mom? Is she okay?"

"Your mom is sick. She is staying in a special place to help her get better."

"Where?"

"Well, she is in a hospital that helps people with mental problems."

"Is she going to be okay?"

"They are taking good care of her, don't worry. Now, are you being treated well and are you happy?"

"Umm, yes."

"Your brother states that you and he sit in the dark on the basement stairs for hours without the ability to go to the bathroom. Your sister said something similar. Is this true? Are you forced to hold it? Do you sit on basement stairs in the dark? No? Are you sure?"

"Yes." I could not look at her face because I knew she would sense I was not being truthful. I kept my eyes focused on the clock on the wall and the ticking of the minute hand.

"Please do not be afraid to answer if this is true. You are safe. Okay? Well, is this true?"

"No."

"Do you eat well? Do you eat what the rest of the family eats?"

"Yes."

"Because that is not what your brother and sister are telling us."

"Yes."

"Are you telling me the truth?"

"Yes."

"You look nervous. Are you telling me the truth?"

"Yes."

"Have you ever seen your sister hit or beaten because she wouldn't eat, or have you ever seen her forced to stay out in the cold?"

My sister's red swollen face was etched so vividly in my mind that I began to feel sick and fought to control my shaking legs.

These questions tore through my heart. I honestly can't believe I was able to say the word "no" when everything inside of me was on the verge of exploding.

"Are you sure?"

"No, I mean yes." I was losing control of my thoughts. I needed to get it out!

"You said no first. Why?"

"You are scaring me."

"I am here to help you. Do you understand that if any of this is true, we can help you?"

When she said this, a face with the signature gap between her teeth flashed before my eyes. "I never saw her being hit or beaten or staying out in the cold." My heart was melting. I loved my sister so.

"Well, have you ever seen your brother being whipped? Have you ever been hit, slapped, or beaten?"

The questions kept building inside of me. I had an answer for them that was begging to be revealed, yet the vault in the recesses of my mind became stronger. Denial surrounded it and I focused on that to get me through it.

"Why are you asking me? I haven't seen anything like that, and I haven't been hit. Please stop asking me!"

"Because we need to know the truth," she said.

"I am telling you the truth! Please leave me alone! I want to go home!" I could tell that she was getting frustrated.

"Okay, just a couple of more questions. Do you get to play? Do you have chores?"

"Yes."

"Yes to what? Do you play?"

"Yes."

"Do you have chores?"

"Yes."

"What kind of chores?"

I stopped answering. She knew I was done talking and I was an emotional wreck. We stood up and she escorted me back down the hallway to my brother and sister. I kept my head down because I didn't want to face my failure. I just wanted to go home to what I knew best. I would not be in trouble and I could continue to live a lie.

The ride home was completely silent; not a word from my sister or brother. I didn't look at them once. This was my opportunity; this was our ticket out! *I denied all of it. I was a broken boy that allowed fear to rule me.*

My brother didn't talk or look at me for a long time after that. How could I blame him? Had I gone along with what was said, would we have been freed? Would they have believed us anyway? Would life in this home have become even worse had I joined the rebellion? Would my brother and sister have left, leaving me to fend for myself? I will never know what the outcome might have been.

We went back to the routine. Nothing changed; at least it didn't get worse. My chores kept me busy. I wondered what happened to my mother and hoped that she would be okay. I still clung to the possibility that someday, maybe, all of us would be back home. My brother eventually forgave me for being a coward. And he remained bound and determined to find a way out.

I Need to Stop!

I thought this was going to help me heal. But the more I type, the more I have guilt. I didn't expect this. It is as though I contributed to their suffering.

I am sorry; this isn't about me.

The story needs to be told. I have waited forty-six years, and I am not going to let the demons dwelling inside the vault win.

Remember that dream? The dream where I was held by a man in a cloud and I couldn't see his face? I know now that it was God Himself. He was letting me know that He was with me and that no matter what happened, He would be there with me. I did not see His face because no one can see His face and live. Can you imagine I was touched by God? I was given this thought by God on January 9, 2014, because He knew I needed it. He gave it to me so I can continue, He gave it to me to give me strength, and He gave it to me to let me know it was not my fault. Most of all, He gave it to me because He loves me. Thank you, Lord, for giving me this blessing. I love you!

Time passed and I continued to hone my skills. My routine consisted of the wind-up alarm clock sounding off, the smell of fresh-brewed coffee, preparing the ham and cheese sandwiches with mustard, filling the thermos, making sure I got the milk and sugar mixture correct and the lunch box packed neatly, dusting and carpet sweeping, loosening the shoelaces, setting out the work boots, waking the family, letting the dog out and feeding him, getting dressed, and then off to school.

After school, there was always scrubbing the kitchen floor, massaging the kitchen cabinets, ironing the T-shirts and underwear in the basement, folding laundry, or whatever chore was assigned for the day. I do not remember the chores my brother or sister did. I focused on my duties. My top priority was to stay in good favor with Janet.

THE BREAKING POINT

As the second summer break rolled around, the thoughts of going back to the cabin sent chills down my spine. We were packed in the usual spot with the summer supplies or on the floorboards. I so desperately wanted the trip to last as long as possible. I tried to feel the road, listening while the tires hummed along the roadway. I counted the left and right turns, anticipating where we might be. I knew when we were on the thruway by the sound of cars passing by and waited for the exit to arrive and the left turn that would lead us through Summersville. As we went by, I wondered what the school, the barn, and the house looked like. I wondered if my mother was in the yard hanging the clothes out to dry and wanted so much to see her beautiful face. I wanted to jump out of the Volkswagen van and run to her. I wanted Rudy to take me on an adventure. I felt a longing for the love I once had as we passed through. I missed them so much.

Descending the steep hill meant that the time was drawing near. Soon, we would be driving the winding paths to the cabin. I knew every twist and turn once we turned off the main road. I can feel the anxiety building up inside me as I type this. The van finally stopped, and the unloading ritual began; we were back in hell.

Because it was raining outside, we sat down at the table inside the cabin and were given oatmeal to eat. I was sitting across from my brother. That day, I was feeling very sick. I must have come down with the flu or something. As I was eating the oatmeal, I started to feel nauseous and vomited the oatmeal back into my bowl. I was so frightened I didn't know what to do. I was afraid of what the consequences would be if I didn't eat. I was afraid to look up at Janet; she was standing in the kitchen watching us. I was hoping against hope for some sympathy. "Eat it," she said.

I glanced at my brother, picked up the spoon, and began eating what I had vomited. I looked up again at my brother, and I saw the rage in his eyes; he lost it. It was the final straw that broke the camel's back. He wasn't about to let his little brother continue to eat vomit.

He sprang from the table and attacked Janet with a vengeance. He smacked her in the face and wrestled with her. Rebecca and I just sat there with our jaws dropped to the floor.

When Janet finally gained control, my brother was locked in the bedroom, and I was back at the table eating my vomit. I hadn't moved a muscle. I could hear Janet telling her husband what had happened. I will never forget what he said. "Get rid of them. Get rid of all of them." What kind of person would say something like that? It was cold and deliberate. I hadn't experienced love for quite some time, and hearing those words really hurt. I felt as though we were nothing. And I still had to finish my oatmeal.

But wait! Those words would turn to joy! What my brother did that day would change our destiny. Mr. Peters meant what he said. My brother did it! He saved us! Well, two of us.

The sequence of events mimicked the last foster home in many ways. A caseworker met with Janet to discuss the transition out while my sister and brother sat quietly in the same room. Funny how they looked so dressed up and neat. Where did those clothes come from? I was tasked with helping pack their belongings and I kept asking myself. *I don't remember seeing any of these clothes on them. Weird!*

Things happened much faster though, a lot faster than our last transition out, literally just a couple of months. It seemed like they were in a rush to get my brother and sister out of the house. I wondered if there was still a cloud hanging over them because of the failed attempt by my brother and sister trying to expose them. Probably … I hope …

My brother and sister would be free from this place. They would be free from living every waking hour not knowing what to expect, living in constant fear. I can't even fathom what went through their minds when they were told they were leaving. I was so happy for them, especially for my sister. They had lived in this home for approximately two years, give or take a couple of months; I do not remember exactly nor do I care to look it up. All I cared about at the time was that they were no longer trapped in this home and were going to a new place, hopefully, a loving place. I did not get a chance to say goodbye to them. Why could I not say goodbye?

I knew Daniel was going to be all right, but I was worried about my sister. I wished that I could have given Rebecca a hug goodbye. I wanted to tell her I loved her and that I was sorry. I wanted to kiss her on the cheek and tell her that she was beautiful. I wanted to hold her, take away her pain, and absorb all of it so she didn't have to carry it with her. *I still do.*

I found out later that the home she moved into took wonderful care of her. They were very loving and kind. I only remember visiting her once. The house was clean and neat. The family had pet birds (one may have been Rebecca's) and, I think, a dog. She looked so beautiful and happy. This is what a little girl deserves: love and affection, being part of the family, sitting at the table next to your foster family that loves you as one of their own, eating the same meal, dessert, and then playtime. I wonder what it was like for her when she finally got these things. She probably cried with joy. I only hope so!

Daniel moved on to a new home. I never visited him there. But one day, I was sitting in class, and a new boy asked me my name. I told him, and he said, "I used to live down the street from a boy named Daniel with your last name." Come to find out it was my brother! Many years later, at age fifty-two, my brother told me that our real dad lived down the street from this foster home. Daniel would visit him all the time, and he eventually moved back home! I couldn't believe it! All these years, I thought my brother lived in foster homes until he turned eighteen or moved out on his own. But he actually moved back home at age fourteen. It just blew my mind that he was back living with my real dad, and I never knew it.

Daniel and I reconnected after I left Janet's foster home. It was so weird that the topic of where he lived after we parted never came up until two years before his death. He called me a week before he passed and told me that he loved me. I often wonder if he knew something and just wanted to share those words with me before he passed. My father died just a year prior and I know this affected my brother. I miss him so much. He was the only sibling that I stayed in contact with throughout my adult life. He was very talented and smart. He could build anything and had just about every tool you could imagine. He graduated from college and was a proud Marine. He did good, considering what our childhood was like.

Hey, Daniel, I love you, brother! I will see you someday, and it will be great! Thank you for taking care of me when we were little. I miss you! I hope you are at peace.

FACING REALITY

Suddenly, I no longer had my brother to look after me. I was on my own. Why didn't I get to leave? The reason was because I conformed. I did what I was told. I never told anyone what went on in the house, and I even protected them from my brother and sister telling the truth. My intense fear and cowardliness played against me. I was the one responsible for staying in this nightmare. Maybe I was being punished for not having the courage to challenge or protect. Maybe I deserved it. I don't know.

The day my brother and sister left it was like starting over. I became more frightened and anxious. Vulnerable. I wanted so badly to be somewhere else that I would even have settled for my second home.

It is hard for me to talk about the three children that belonged to the Peters. I had had very little direct interaction with them up to this point. I continued my cleaning duties in the morning before school and after I got home. I tried to stay unnoticed by keeping to my chores and staying quiet. I wouldn't speak unless spoken to and looked forward to the ironing duties in the basement.

One day I was asked, "Would you be interested in being adopted by us?" I couldn't believe my ears! Janet wanted me to be her son! I was only eleven or twelve years old, but I certainly knew what that meant. It was okay to torture my sister, abuse my brother, and allow me to be humiliated and beaten, yet she wanted me to be part of her family? This was the first time I stood up for myself. Even if I had to finish out my childhood years in this place, there was absolutely no way I was going to be made a part of their family. Do you think if I had said yes that would have changed the way I was treated? Would it wipe away the pain and suffering and bring love and acceptance as an equal member of the family? I think not! There was nothing to wipe away.

I was frightened out of my wits when I said no, because I didn't conform. What was my fate going to be now? I was glad that I said no, and when I saw the look on Janet's face, a look of rejection and total shock, well, it felt good. She immediately sent me to the third level to scrub and wax the linoleum floor. I spent the entire Saturday on the third level but for some reason, this punishment was a pleasure. I won this little battle because in my mind, she didn't get her wish—and trust me, this chore wasn't new to me. I had control for just a minute or two, and no matter what happened in the future, I still had a mom and a dad somewhere in this world that belonged to me.

DAD'S VISITS

My mother never visited the home. I only saw her the one time downtown and then didn't see her again until later in life when I was on my own. I remember rushing to the hospital to try and see her before she passed, but I was too late. I was allowed a few minutes alone with her. I held her tight praying to God to please take care of her and give her new life and a beautiful mind. That was the closest I ever felt to my mother. She was still warm when I was holding her. I was afraid to let go since this would be the last time that I would hold her.

I had my mom for a few moments. I blamed my father for her sickness and years of living in the mental hospital. I was angry and sad at the same time. I loved my mom even though I never really knew her. It wasn't her fault. I hope someday we will be together. Sorry, I am wandering again but I will never forget that moment.

I can count on my fingers the number of visits that my father showed up to see me over the years. Janet and her sister were always there whenever I saw him. I am assuming that it was one of those deals where someone had to be present in the room (you know, the so-called supervised visits). The meetings would always take place in the eat-in kitchen area while the two onlookers constantly stared at us. Janet's sister would wear her miniskirts and sit opposite my father just to tease him.

Dad had a red, bloodshot nose and watery eyes. When he sat down next to me and began to speak, I was taken back in time. That smell that I longed for when I was in my second and third home was mixed with every breath he took. His Southern drawl was slurred by the amount of alcohol pumping through his veins. He put his arms around me and hugged me tight. Even after all this time and the fact that I was older, I was anticipating a nibble on my ear. How sad was that! I barely knew the man sitting beside me. All I had was the memories of a three-year-old child.

My father would whisper to me so the intruders couldn't hear what he was saying. He asked if I loved him, and I said, "Yes." He asked me if I missed him, and I said, "Yes." He asked me if I was happy living in this home, and I said, "Yes." He asked me a lot of questions that made him feel better.

I didn't ask why he never came to see me or why he didn't help Mom. I didn't ask why he never took us back home so we could be a family. I didn't ask if he loved me too. I wanted to ask, but I didn't. I didn't want to hurt him.

I sat next to a broken man who came to see me in a drunken state, and when the hour was finished, he would give me a hug and leave. I did not know who he was. I felt sorry for him.

The visits deepened the emptiness inside me. I began to realize that I would never be rescued from this place. I would never go home. The fantasy that played out so often in my mind would never come to pass. I was trapped now, and there was little hope for a normal life. The rest of the visits were very similar. Dad needed to feel better about himself, and I needed to do what I do best, comply!

THE THIRD LEVEL

I haven't opened the pages in this manuscript for a while now. I was thinking about what is coming next. What will happen when people who know me read my darkest secrets? Will I be supported? Will they think of me differently? Will they say that I am not normal? Will they turn away and talk about me behind my back? Will I be embarrassed? Yes! But I am who I am, and there is no changing or erasing what happened. My upbringing has made me who I am today. I need to continue my story.

I was reaching the age of twelve and something was wrong. I was not growing. I was at the bottom of all the growth-indicator charts. Janet took me to see a specialist at the hospital to undergo a bunch of tests. The results revealed that I was four years behind in my growth. How could that be? I was twelve years old and had the bone structure of a nine-year-old. Wow! There wasn't a speck of hair growth below the waistline either. I was obviously self-conscious to begin with, having my pants pulled down by my foster aunt.

The doctors recommended that I undergo hormone therapy, but I refused. I had control of my own body! Some of you may know that back in those days, we used to have to swim naked in the pool at school. I was in great physical shape (I will get into that later), but still I had no pubic hair. How embarrassing! Just so you know, I turned out all right and I would eventually get my man hair.

A new foster brother arrived. His name was William. I liked him from the beginning, and we got along well. Foster children seem to have a silent connection. We know what it feels like to be shuffled from home to home. We are reunited and then separated from siblings. We are told that it is only temporary until our parents get the help that they need and we live in endless hope that this may soon come true. The reality is that for me, for William, and for so many others, that hope fades to distant memories.

With Daniel gone, I had learned to protect myself. The only thing that made me feel safe in the beginning was to keep busy with the chores. William soon joined me. I tried to help him stay out of trouble. He endured many of the same punishments that I did. Pleasing Janet was the main objective for both of us. William had to learn the hard way as was the norm, but he was a lot like me. He wanted to please and stay out of trouble.

The middle boy started a delivery route for the *Buffalo Evening News*. I was given the "opportunity" to help him deliver the newspapers. This was a great escape for me as I would be out of the house and free to roam the streets. I eventually learned the route by heart and took it over. I was amazed that I could do this on my own. William would eventually become my helper. God was shining on us when this happened. We were both free for a bit and had fun. We made many adult friends that treated us like normal children.

I will never forget this one family that would take us in on cold winter days to let us warm up. These people were very small in stature. They were a husband and wife that had a deformity in their spinal area. We were offered hot cocoa and socks for William to wear since he had to endure the rubber boots with no socks on many occasions. We would drop the socks off before heading home. We had better make it home within a certain time period or we would be in big trouble. Excuses did not exist. I remember seeing this elderly couple drive slowly by our house many times. I think they wanted to make sure we were okay.

As it so happened, the oldest boy decided to have a paper route, so the *Courier Express* entered the picture. Before long, I would be up at 5:30 a.m., delivering the courier express newspaper and doing all the other chores prior to school. I prayed that I wouldn't oversleep because there would be hell to pay. I set an alarm clock every night to make sure I wouldn't hear that "Jacob, wake up and get moving now!" voice that would happen on rare occasions. If I didn't get up, everyone in the household was thrown off track. I hated the responsibility.

The neat thing about the paper routes was that they followed the same route, so many of the customers were the same people. I loved collecting the money. I got many tips and stashed the savings in the battery compartment of a radio that I had stuffed in the back of the closet under some clothes so no one would find it. The money grew over the years. I was shocked at how much I had when it all ended. William and I enjoyed many treats along the way too. We were safe for a bit or so we thought.

The Third Level: This is where innocence is lost. This is where the child is manipulated and demons are born into existence.

The third level was the bedroom area for the two oldest boys, William and I. The stairway was protected from the third-level floor by spindles that tied into the ceiling. To the right was a set of bunk beds, a closet, and the entrance into the half attic. To the left was a single bed, another closet, dresser drawers, and plenty of flooring for William to sleep on.

One Saturday afternoon, while performing my laundry duties, I approached the top of the stairwell. I glanced to my right and saw the oldest boy facing the open closet with his pants around his ankles. He was doing something with his hand in front of him. He did not notice me because he was focused on what he was doing. I quietly slipped back down the stairs and left the room. I had never witnessed anything like that and wondered what he was doing. I know what you are thinking. No, I hadn't discovered myself yet, even at the age of twelve.

The third level was not exempt from my cleaning duties. As I had mentioned earlier, I spent many a day scrubbing and waxing the tile flooring. I would also have to clean and organize the closets and the attic area. Part of my laundry duties included gathering the dirty clothing from the third level as well as restocking the clean clothing.

I noticed that the closet area where the oldest boy was standing had many soiled socks that were thrown in the back of the closet. I would eventually figure out what was going on, and I kept it to myself. I would retrieve them and add them to the laundry. What else was I supposed to do? By the way, if I didn't have a pair of matched socks, I had to hunt them down. I didn't let this bother me and focused on my duties.

It wasn't long after my brother and sister left that the oldest boy began to take notice of me. He would ask me questions about school and my schoolmates and say how strong my body looked. I was tinkering with a weight set in the basement without anyone knowing about it. I felt good about my interaction with him because I was finally being considered as a possible foster brother. What is a foster brother? Is it someone who you can relate to as being your brother in some way? Is it someone that you would consider protecting you in times of trouble? Is it someone that you would want to consider a part of your real family? Many foster children would like to think so, and many foster children would love the idea of having someone that they could connect to in such a way. I felt this with Rudy. He was and still is my brother. I am sure that he feels the same way.

I began to interact more with the middle boy. For some reason, I felt comfortable with him. He gave me his .22 caliber Sears and Roebuck rifle as a gift and a crucifix of Jesus that I had discovered in the closet to the left of the stairs. The crucifix touched my heart and I found comfort in holding it. I would retrieve it many times when I felt lost, just to look at it. Almost five decades later, I still have the .22 rifle, and the crucifix of Jesus is hanging on my bedroom wall in my country home. I look at it before I go to sleep and every morning when I wake.

The youngest boy connected with William. I witnessed conversation that seemed to be normal, and I thought this was good for William. William and I thought that we were finally, maybe, being looked upon by the foster boys as foster brothers.

Andrew arrived in the house next. He had Down's syndrome. I attached myself to him immediately. His job was to sit on a potty chair from sunup to sundown. I felt terrible for him. It was my job to constantly inspect his potty chair for signs of movement. He couldn't speak normally and was always forcing his thick tongue out and wetting his lips. He was good at giving great big hugs, and I enjoyed hugging him. Every now and then I would rub his bottom because I knew it was bothering him. He craved attention and received little. I loved Andrew. I wanted to free him from his shackles. I wanted to see him walking, playing, and hugging. I wanted him to be loved. I loved him.

There would be many new arrivals, babies with burn marks from cigarette butts and babies that were neglected or unwanted by their parents. I loved taking care of them. I learned how to prepare the milk, making sure it wasn't too hot on my wrist. I changed many a diaper and enjoy every minute of it. I remember one day I poked through a belly button with a bobby pin and thought I was going to die! The baby was fine, but I made sure that it didn't happen again.

I used cloth diapers and bobby pins. This meant plunging and removing the poop in the toilet. I learned to do this without gagging. God has his way of preparing us for the future. I would have no problem dipping my hands into the toilet to perform this duty. I loved taking care of the babies. I loved putting them to bed and watching them sleep so peacefully.

Sleep was not so peaceful for me. My bed was the top bunk bed to the right of the stairwell. I would lie quietly in bed clenching the stale pillow and focus on faint shadows that cast strange images across the room. I would not fall asleep until all was silent as people slipped into a quiet slumber. *I am safe.*

Suddenly, I was awakened by the oldest boy. He crawled under the sheets and lay next to me. He took his hand and placed it between my legs. I was in total shock and lay motionless. He whispered in my ear, "Do not be afraid. I am going to take your underwear off." He descended to my privates and said, "My, you have gotten a lot bigger!" He put his mouth over my penis and began to move up and down. He stopped for a moment and said, "This is how I want you to do it." He reversed the position and forced my head down between his legs.

I was told to do as he did. I was unable to defend myself and did what he asked. Again, he stopped me for a moment and said that something was going to come in my mouth, and I was to swallow it. He said it would not hurt me. When it happened, he forced my head down until it was over. I held it in my mouth and spat it into the bedding. He didn't say a word and left the bed. I wasn't dreaming.

Now you know: now everyone knows. I was taken by a person that was supposed to be a brother figure, a protector, and a friend. I will live with this injustice until the day I die. This act solidified the vault. I became a prisoner of self-denial, of shame, of embarrassment, but most of all, I lost who I was. I was no longer a child who was innocent and clean. My soul bore a deep scar that could never be healed, and there would be more to come. I trusted no one from that point on. But I stayed quiet, not telling a soul.

I had a new threat that I was not prepared for. I had lost the sanctuary of my bed. The one place in my childhood that I felt safe and prayed to get to just so I could feel safe was now my worst fear. I began contemplating suicide again. I had so many ways that I was going to end my miserable life, I could write a book on it (no pun intended). The thought of being trapped and forced to do that act again was unbearable.

Then I replaced suicidal thoughts with denial. I pretended that it didn't happen. I pretended to be normal, and I pretended to show the oldest boy that what he did was not going to bother me. I was very good at blocking it out during the daytime hours. Schoolmates would never know, and my paper routes gave me the freedom to participate in a normal world. When William and I came home from delivering the papers, I would work feverishly on my chores.

The world of sexual deviance lurked in the dark shadows of the third level. It would show itself in other parts of the house when the parents weren't home. I began to sense when it was coming and whom it was coming for. My eyes and ears honed in on the sounds of the darkness, the quiet whispers of someone calling you in the night. I would hide my face under the sheets, trying to breath in the smell of the stale pillow as I strained to see who was coming. This was how I learned that I wasn't alone. I wasn't the only victim.

What went through my mind when I saw William being told to do what I had to do? It was the middle boy that forced him to do it, not the oldest boy that had taken me. This sick sexual world was unfolding right before my eyes. As I have mentioned, William was a lot like me, and he did what he was told. What on earth was wrong with us? Why didn't we fight?

I didn't think William knew that I was taken by the oldest boy when I caught him performing oral sex on the middle boy. He was embarrassed when I caught him and said that he knew that I was doing it too. Of course, I denied it. I was trying to protect myself from being branded. What was going on in our minds? William needed to know that he wasn't alone in this unthinkable act. He needed proof that I was also part of this. I could understand why he needed that, but I didn't want him to know. I didn't want to be exposed.

The soiled socks continued to pile up in the back of the closet. They would soon be accompanied by soiled T-shirts and stains on all sorts of items located in the storage area of the half attic. The youngest boy had now discovered himself. I felt dirty everywhere I turned. Was he going to take the next step and join his brothers?

The sound of the alarm clock no longer taunted me; it became my friend. It meant that I made it through the night and could now focus on my regimented morning chores. The morning rituals gave me comfort. I was a well-oiled machine. I could almost perform my tasks blindfolded, and I was proud of my accomplishments. The morning air, physical exercise from pulling the wagon, and a slice of freedom before school helped me morph into the tough guy as soon as I stepped onto the bus. I would block out the dark thoughts and disgusting visions. William was my partner, and he too was trying to stay hidden from being exposed. Our secret was safe from the outsiders, and we were desperate to keep it that way.

I met a boy, Tony, that lived one street over. He would help William and me deliver papers after school. It was ironic that this boy had bright red hair just like Rudy. He became a good friend and somehow managed to become a frequent visitor at the house. The foster parents allowed Tony to enter my realm of after-school duties. He helped me with a lot of things and would eventually play a key role in helping me become stronger both physically and emotionally. He was shielded from the dark side (I made sure of that).

Back to the babies: much of my time was focused on taking care of the new babies that would temporarily stay at the house. I loved taking care of them! It didn't matter what they needed. I was always happy to do whatever it took to make them feel loved. Preparing the pabulum was the trickiest part. It must not be too thick or too runny, too hot or too cold. I wouldn't put it in their mouth until it was just right. Holding them was the best part. They needed love and so did I.

It was these precious little babies that gave me hope. I was able to give and receive love in a normal way through them. God was using them to help me. He gave me these special gifts because He knew I needed them, and they needed me.

CABINREVISITED

When summer break started to creep ever so closer, I began to have thoughts of what awaited me. I felt sick inside at the thought of going back to the cabin. The fact that my brother and sister were no longer in the picture didn't make it any easier for me. I was still vulnerable. I was certain that William was feeling it too. He had never been to the cabin before but knowing what went on in the house, spending time at a secluded cabin with the three brothers must have weighed heavily on his thoughts. Though I had endured three years of this myself, it still made me sick just thinking about the cabin in the woods.

The same rituals of packing, sitting in our designated spot, the sounds, the scenery, and landmarks that I would envision in my mind, a beautiful woman, the hill, and then the wooded darkness. The only good thing was that the oldest boy slept in the cabin, and we would sleep in the van. On occasion, Tony would join us. I felt safer when he was around because I was sure that his presence would hinder any plans that might have been in store for me.

On one of the outings to the cabin, a friend of the middle boy came along. The middle boy and his friend had pitched a tent out in the clearing. I was walking by and heard the friend talking to William. As I got closer, my heart began to pound. The friend was taunting him. My senses were heightening, and my legs began to tremble. I could hear what was being said. William was being forced to do our secret to an outsider. I sat down in the grass and began to cry. I felt hopeless, and now he was being attacked outside of the family group.

As I sat there, I wondered if I was going to be exposed. I didn't want to live like this anymore. I didn't want to see someone else being abused anymore. How could I stop it? At that moment, I looked up and focused my eyes on the bright sun. If I stared at it long enough, I would go blind! I thought this would save me from seeing the evil that surrounded us. I looked at it until I could no longer see except for a glow around the outer edges of my eyes. As I stood up, I tried to look at the trail that led to the cabin. I began to panic because I could not see. What had I done? I could still hear what was going on in the tent, and now I wasn't able to move. How stupid! I did not make anything better; I made it worse.

I closed my eyes and sat back down. I cupped my hands over my ears and began to say the prayer that my mom in Summersville had taught me. I kept my eyes closed and repeated the prayer over and over. I did not open my eyes for a long time. I eventually removed my hands from over my ears and listened. All that I could hear were the sounds of nature; still I kept my eyes closed. The tent was silent. They must have gone somewhere and didn't see me.

Am I blind? The thought of being blind now hit me. Why did I do this? I could still hear the evil, but now I wouldn't be able to see it coming. How stupid of me. With my eyes still closed, I rose to my feet. I thought about God and asked him to help me. Why is it that we think very little about God until we are in trouble? I slowly opened one eye and then the other. I began to panic because all I saw was a dark brown hazy glow and could barely make out the trees and the path to the cabin. What was I going to tell Janet? I began to walk toward the cabin with terrible thoughts of what my life was going to be like now. I had done this to myself.

I sat back down and asked God once again to help me. I closed my eyes and again began to pray. I prayed all sorts of things. I promised I would be good. I promised I would take good care of the little babies. I promised that I would forgive people, and I promised not to hurt anyone. There were a host of prayers that didn't make sense, but I said them anyway. I wanted to see. I didn't really know God, but I was hoping that He was listening.

I stood up and opened my eyes. I could still barely see the images in front of me. I just stood there with my eyes facing the cabin. I was motionless, looking straight ahead, trying to focus. I noticed that the longer I kept my eyes open, the brown haze began to fade a bit. After a while, I was able to see objects and make out the trail to the cabin. I began to walk slowly, fixating on the cabin. I started worrying about the voice that was inevitable, calling me to begin my chores again. The longer I walked, the clearer my vision. By the time I reached the concrete patio, I was able to make out just about everything. The brown haze that covered the center of my eyes was fading.

I said nothing and was able to make it to my slumber in the van without anyone knowing what I did. William lay next to me. I didn't say a word about what happened. I wanted to let him to know how bad I felt, but I thought it would be better for him if I said nothing. I knew what that disgusting act did inside, and I didn't want him to be even more humiliated. I could sense that he thought that I knew something. We just lay there silently and fell asleep.

I woke up the next day and could see clearly. I had averted yet another stupid plan to save myself from the trap I was in. As for William, he was back to being himself. When a person is constantly being abused, the mind can block the event for a short period of time, as if it didn't happen. The memory just takes its place in the vault, only to be revealed whenever it wants to show itself. We cannot keep it in the vault without experiencing the event over and over in our minds. The disgusting acts live on forever. The vault keeps them hidden, but it also preserves them. As for my eyes, I had twenty/eighteen vision up until age forty. Did God take care of me? I think we know the answer to that question, don't we?

As the days passed, I began to fear that I too might have been exposed to the outside world. If

William was taken by an outsider, then what was to stop the oldest boy or the outsider from telling someone? What if the outsider wanted me! I became obsessed with what William was doing. When one of the three boys were on the third level, I would find myself drawn to the stairs. It didn't matter what I was doing. I would find a way to slip to the bottom of the stairwell to listen. I felt sick inside and didn't quite understand why I needed to find out what might happen to William. It was like I was trying to justify my own actions with the oldest boy even though it didn't make any logical sense. I was nauseous just thinking about it.

I didn't want William to be abused. Maybe catching him in the act would stop them? Why didn't I say anything to my foster parents? I was certain that they would deny any wrongdoing by their sons and especially something as perverse as sexual abuse. I would also bet that I would have been punished. I didn't say a word to anyone. Not for decades.

It was late in the afternoon on a Saturday. The foster parents were out, and the oldest boy was at home. He called me to the third level. He was alone, and I had no idea where the other two boys were. William was downstairs doing chores. When I heard the voice calling me, I knew what was going to happen. I climbed the stairwell praying that I might be wrong and that the boy needed me for something else. When I got to the top of the stairs, he was lying on the bottom bunk bed with the sheets pulled down exposing his naked body. He told me to take off my clothes and lie next to him. This is where the mind begins to work to protect you. I pretended that I was somewhere else. I could hear him telling me what to do, and I did it, but it wasn't me doing it, right?

He was telling me to do some new things. I just did it because I was afraid. "Lick between my legs, and lick my__________s." Again, I was trying desperately to be in another place when I was doing this. I was trying my best to not feel, hear, taste, or smell anything. I tried to pull the sheets over me, but he would pull them back so he could watch me. I couldn't breathe and was gasping for air. I honestly cannot believe that I am typing this. I am no longer protected, and it scares me to death!

As I was down between his legs, I heard the door to the bottom of the stairwell open. I tried to make it to the pillow next to the oldest boy before the person reached the top of the stairs. It was William. He had caught me in the act. I tried to deny it, but we were both naked lying next to each other. William now knew that he was not alone. He could use this against me whenever he wanted to. In his mind, we were now partners, and there was no denying it. I was now living in fear of being exposed by William.

He was probably doing the exact same thing that I was. He was listening at the bottom of the stairway just as I did. It sickened me that we had to try and justify our guilt. We both knew that we had to live with what we did. Trying to minimize it by catching each other in the act only made it worse. I will never understand this; it doesn't make any sense!

When William left the room, I got out of the bed. I refused to continue with the oldest boy. What was my fate going to be now? Would he say anything to other people, to the outsiders?

Weeks passed, and William said nothing. It was like we were okay knowing that we had this common bond, this disgusting secret. I never heard a word from the brothers or anyone outside the family about what I had done. The outsider was not aware of what I had done. He kept his encounter with William to himself. He did not know that I was outside the tent back at the cabin, and I told no one about it either.

I looked for ways to push the demons back that were constantly taunting me. There was that plastic weight set and some dumbbells that I tinkered with in the past sitting idle in the basement that belonged to one to the brothers. I was now in my mid-teens and decided to try lifting some weights when given the opportunity. I still had my routine: the morning chores, newspaper routes, taking care of the babies, and watching over poor Andrew.

I was very good at timing a quick run to the basement to pick up the weights and exercise. I had no idea what I was doing and struggled with proper technique to gain strength. I soon had my redheaded friend helping me. I began to see results quickly and was eventually given permission to workout for a short period of time.

THE FINAL BATTLE

was in the third level area, and the oldest boy ascended the stairs. It was late in the evening on a Saturday. He approached me and drew me close to him. I began to panic and something inside me snapped! I was about sixteen years old and wasn't going to let this happen to me again. I fought with everything I had and broke away from him. I ran to the top of the stairs, ready to descend, when the door opened. It was Janet. Still in panic mode, I yelled out, "I am going to tell Mom what you made me do." I never called her Mom.

She just looked at me. She didn't ask me "what did he make you do?" She just closed the door. What did that mean? I flew down the stairs, went straight to the basement, and worked out until I could no longer move. No one stopped me. No one came to talk to me. I was on my own, but I had won a significant battle. There was only one reason that I was allowed to do this. She must have known something.

After this happened, I was given more freedom to spend time with my redheaded friend. Janet must have had a sense of fear that I might have enough courage to tell someone about the sexual abuse and everything else that my eyes had witnessed. I was so ashamed that I failed to do just that. Even as a teenager, I kept silent. I could not bear the thought of being exposed. I pushed my sister back in the vault and kept her there. I let William struggle with the boys and didn't stop it. I lost touch with what was right and lived in a pretend state of mind. I must live with the fact that I could have changed other people's lives and made their future somewhat normal. Is there strength in being a coward? I think not.

I focused on getting stronger and enjoyed the reputation that I was getting in school though I didn't flaunt my bodybuilding. I was lucky to find another close friend who needed some encouragement. I helped him transform his body and gave him confidence and self-pride. I saw a positive change in him that he carried throughout our friendship. I did something good for someone, and it felt good for a change. We remained good friends. Tony the redhead was still in there, pumping me up. I even got William to pick up some weights. He would always show me his biceps. They were looking good!

By the time I was a junior in high school my body was in top physical condition. I hadn't had the freedom outside of school to really consider dating. I did, however, have the desire to. I had little experience in speaking with girls and was very shy. I was also afraid to get close to any of them. Having someone in my life that cared about me frightened me for several reasons. What if she wanted to touch me or hold me? What if she started asking questions about my family? What if she said she wanted to meet my parents? But the worst fear I had was what if I really liked this person and she rejected me because I couldn't open up and be like the other guys who had a normal family? I didn't have what my classmates had. I decided to wait for a while.

William and I stopped trying to catch each other in the act, mostly because I had finally broken away from the oldest boy, and I had freedom to do things that were somewhat normal. I had also started to work part-time for my next-door neighbor, performing cleaning duties for an industrial company.

One late afternoon, I had finished my cleaning early and came home. I opened the door to the third level and hopped up the steps, skipping over some of them. When I reached the top, I found William lying on his stomach and the youngest boy was on top of him. There was a jar of petroleum jelly next to them. I turned and ran back down the stairs. I felt such rage inside. Mr. Peters was sitting in his usual spot, and I walked up to him, blocking his view from the television. He looked at me and said, "What's your problem?"

If you have ever lifted weights, you will understand what every muscle in my body was doing. I wanted to pick him up from that stupid recliner and drag him upstairs to the third level. I was seventeen now; I could speak out and tell him what I just witnessed. I could say what a failure he was as a parent. I could have said enough is enough, and I was going

to open the floodgates and tell everyone about everything. But I didn't. I turned and left the room, once
again the coward.

I waited for William to say something to me, but
he never did. I found it so difficult to comprehend
that all three boys were doing this to innocent children. This home was filled with sick people and sexual desires that would scar even the toughest person.

BREAKING FREE

I want out! After witnessing what happened to William, I started to think about ways of getting out of the house for good. I was hoping for some miracle to happen but knew I was going to have to get through my senior year before I had any chance of leaving. William, I, and Andrew had to hang in there.

I was asked to help put together a newsletter that Janet had written. The main body of the letter was having group discussions with parents in need of help. Parents would get together to discuss the many problems associated with raising their children. They would talk about child abuse and neglect. They would meet in various locations, and I would have the task of looking after the children in another room. I would have help from other adults as the groups increased in size.

I was amazed at how quickly this organization grew. We were doing newsletters all the time, and I picked people up and drove them home after I got my license.

Janet, who did unspeakable things to us, was now helping others cope with bringing their children up in their own families, so the kids did not end up in foster care. God has his way of working through people. This organization helped many parents, and Janet was the key player in making it happen. She needs to get credit for what she did to help others. The physical and emotional scars, however, that my brother and sister endured can never be taken back. The physical and emotional scars that the other foster children, including William and Andrew, sustained can never be taken back. They are real, and they happened. I wish I knew what Janet was thinking when she was pictured as a savior of parenting while knowing deep inside what she, her husband, children, and sister did to me.

Finishing my senior year and graduating brought me one step closer to my goal of finding my freedom. I also began a roller-coaster ride with the girls. I dated several girls at once, not because I was trying to be a stud but because if I lost one, then I still had another that cared about me. I hurt some beautiful people because of this, and it still bothers me. I am so very sorry for that. I wasn't capable of expressing true love and focused on the what-if instead of what was going on in the minds of these thoughtful, loving women. I was afraid of losing what I had because that was all that I knew. Selfish in my actions, it was a terrible feeling waking up every day wondering if I would lose something close to me. If I could only find those women today, I would give them this book to read. Maybe, just maybe, they would understand and forgive. I often wonder about them.

I took a little nap after typing the last few pages. I had a dream that brought me back to the third-level stairwell. I was facing downward with a bowl of hot soup cradled in my hands. My hands were draped with a towel to protect me from the heat. Daniel was standing just below me, ready to accept the bowl of soup. He also had his hands protected with a towel. I felt a negative presence behind me. It was the middle boy that my brother hated with such passion. As I was handing over the soup, the middle boy tried to tip it over onto my brother. I struggled to stop it and was successful. I then looked at Daniel and knew what he wanted to do. I stared into his eyes and said, "Don't do it. Please don't do it." He just looked at me and smiled.

Something came over me, and I felt the need to show my brother that I had courage, something I never did outside of my dreams. I threw the bowl of hot soup over my shoulders and onto the middle boy. He vanished in an instant. My brother vanished too. Then the youngest boy entered the dream and proceeded to tell me the things I would have to replace because the soup had ruined his boots and clothing that were sitting on the stairs. Janet showed up and handed me a scrub brush and bucket and walked away without uttering a word. I cleaned the stairs from top to bottom; then I woke up.

I am sixty-one years old now, and I still dream of these things. I quit trying to analyze the dreams a long time ago. They can mean so many different things. A psychiatrist would have fun with this one.

During my first year of college, I was constantly thinking of ways to leave this home. The paper routes were a faded memory, and I was still working as a part-time cleaner. The money that I had stashed in the battery compartment while delivering newspapers was still there. I had never counted the exact amount and kept it tucked away. The money that I was getting for cleaning helped to maintain a beat-up Dodge Dart, and I had to pay my foster father for the insurance. The car was in his name.

I decided to take a chance and move in with my boss. He was so kind. It was he that asked if I wanted to stay with him. He lived directly across the street and though I didn't ask or share, I can guarantee he saw things that made him question our safety. I was so thankful yet so frightened to leave. Packing my belongings and walking out the door felt so strange. It was like a magnet was drawing me back into the house. I kept thinking I was letting people down and I was worried about the safety of others in the house.

When I moved in, I was emotionally confused. I was lost and not comforted by the new surroundings. I was only at my boss' place for about two weeks when I was told by my foster father to return the car or he would take it because it was in his name. He was angry that I left. I am certain that Janet was pulling his strings once again. I had to go back and face him. I could not go to school without the car, and it really didn't legally belong to me. I had to go back; I had no choice. About a month later, I thought about the money in the battery compartment and decided to see how much I had. I counted nine hundred dollars!

I couldn't believe that I had that much money. I was seeing a wonderful woman at the time, and she was willing to help me. She worked for the same company that I did. She was a beautiful blue-eyed soft-spoken woman and she took my breath away. She wanted me to move in with her and that got my attention quickly! We had our plan. So, I bought a truck for the exact amount of nine hundred dollars. This woman helped me with getting the insurance and the truck in my name. I will forever be grateful for her kindness. Without her help, I would have had to wait even longer before I could leave. You have no idea what I was feeling inside, anticipating a final break from this home.

With the truck on the road, I went immediately to the house. I quickly filled the back of the truck with everything I could claim to be mine. I did not say a word to anyone in the house, not one word. All I could think about was, this was it! I would be free from the silent demons that constantly challenged my conscience as I climbed the stairwell to the third level, free from the kitchen and behind the door, free from the basement and the shadows of the stairway, free from encountering the three brothers, and free from the anxiety of facing William and Andrew, wondering and hoping that they were okay. I would be free from it all!

And so, I left: but I wasn't free. I would never be free. I felt guilty for abandoning William and Andrew. I felt guilty for abandoning my duties. I even felt guilty that I might have hurt Janet and my foster father. I carry the guilt of my sister and my brother and all the secrets. It will never go away. It is part of my being. It shaped the person that I am today. I hide my demons well. I care deeply for others, and I try to please everyone. I try to be the best at what I do so others see me as successful. I try not to hurt anyone, and when I do, I struggle to make it right. I must do well. I must *comply*.

What do people always say about children who have been abused? They will most likely grow up and do the same thing to their spouse or children? This is just an excuse for those who take the wrong path in life. God gives us the gift of free will. We make the choice to do good or evil. Does it make sense to hurt someone that you brought into this word just because it happened to you? We are all inherently good, and I think most of us want to make children feel loved, not cause them to face the same demons that we did.

I have made many, many mistakes in my life. However, I do know this: I never intentionally tried to hurt someone to make me feel better. I have suffered to make others feel good. There is good in suffering for others; look what Jesus did for us! I took the right path, and I know who is guiding me.

LIFE BEGINS

Moving in with this beautiful woman and having my own place was like a dream come true. I was working for the same company and was promoted to production equipment mechanic. I had a knack for repairing industrial sewing machines. I also attended college to become a male nurse and worked around a challenging schedule. My beautiful live-in partner worked at the same company; that was how we met. I worked second shift and went to school during the day. This schedule did not help my relationship.

I found friendship with a workmate that enjoyed a bit of drink. I would slip away and wander across the street with my buddy and settle down at a barstool. I was not used to drinking and my body wasn't either. It didn't take very long for this to change. My drinking buddy and I would have liquid lunches almost every evening and then head over to the bar after work. We would each put down four pounders during lunch breaks. This self-centered behavior did not go over well with my girlfriend. I was not myself when I was drinking. Who is?

She was such an amazing person. She had the bluest eyes, the brightest smile, and the sweetest, softest voice that could capture your attention in a heartbeat. Pregnant with my child, she put up with my unfaithfulness, stupidity, and selfishness for as long as she could but eventually reached a breaking point and asked me to leave. I began to panic because once again I had lost something that I thought I truly loved. I was programmed to think that I would lose those that I loved and now I had to live with the fact that I had done this to myself. I mention that a lot, don't I? "I did this to myself." I deserved it. She helped me find another apartment.

On June 7, 1980, my son was born. This changed my way of thinking. I wanted to be a good dad. I knew what it was like to not have a father and I was determined to make sure my son felt his father's love. I loved him the moment I set eyes on him. I was devastated when his mom announced that she was moving away when he was six months old. She had found a well-paying job and she had family out that way, so it certainly made sense. But I was not going to let distance deter me from seeing him. I would get in my car and pick him up on the weekends and summer breaks. I never missed a child support payment and paid half the medical bills. I needed to show my son and myself that I was a responsible and loving dad. His mom and I got along well. She was (and still is) a beautiful mom. I never had to worry.

My son and I have an amazing bond. He is so smart and talented and has done very well for himself. We often communicate on projects and share ideas on how to go about getting them done properly. I so enjoy this. He has a beautiful wife and I am blessed with two awesome granddaughters and another is on the way!

When my son was settled in a new town and I was living on my own I found myself looking for love. I dated several women and fell into the same fear-of-losing cycle. I had to have a backup. I finally came to my senses and ended up involved in another serious relationship. She eventually moved in and we began a sometimes wonderful, sometimes rocky romance. She was feisty and loved to dance. I started to get my body back into shape and set up a weight room in the mobile home that I had purchased.

We spent a lot of time at her parents' house. They were so much fun to be around. Her father was a great cook and we would have an occasional beer together on the front porch. She was very close to her parents. It was good to see them together. She had brothers and sisters that lived on the same street that made family visits a common theme. I admired their love for one another.

We would visit the cabin and the lake to try and break the chains that bound me. This woman in my life at the time had no idea. It was just a fun day for her.

As the years passed, I began to question my feelings and wondered where I was headed in life. I felt uneasy in my relationship but did not share this with my partner as I should have. I did not give her the opportunity to help me change what I was feeling inside. I should have confided in her, but I didn't. My thoughts turned to yet another woman.

This woman, you guessed it, also worked at my place of employment. She was much younger than me, pretty and petite. I honestly cannot remember how we ended up in each other's arms, but I fell in love with her right from the start. I had never felt this kind of love before. When it happened, I was determined to begin my life by finally doing things right. I wanted to get married, have children, and live how God intended a marriage to be.

Do things right? Well, not exactly. A bombshell hit. "I am pregnant." No, not the person I fell in love with but the person I was separating from. I had to let that sink in. I was going to be a father again. I was going to have a second child out of wedlock. I searched my heart and made the difficult decision to keep to my original dream. I could not deny the fact that I was deeply in love with someone else. I can't imagine how difficult this must have been for her.

There would be terrible days and months ahead as we battled our way through the breakup. I would follow through with my marriage and my wife would become pregnant! So, I had two women pregnant just months apart. In a short burst, two precious little girls were born into this world. Arguments, bumps, and bruises lingered as we worked through visitation schedules and child support. Time would eventually calm things down. My ex would find a man totally dedicated to her and our daughter and love would fill her heart.

I know what you are thinking. Here is a man that had children by three different women, two out of wedlock. I made many mistakes in my life, but I can tell you this: my children are not one of them. If you were to ask my children today, they would tell you how much they love one another. This is because of the selfless dedication of all three women. They put their differences aside and focused on what mattered most. They wanted their children to be bound tight, grounded in the kind of love that only siblings share. They succeeded beyond my wildest dreams.

In a few short years my wife would become pregnant again. We were blessed with a beautiful baby boy. As he began to grow, we noticed things were a bit off. He was having difficulties rolling onto his stomach. There were many visits to the doctors and a hospital stay for failure to thrive. He had difficulties in sitting up and crawling, lacked steadiness when standing while holding our hands, failed to respond to noises, and made little eye contact. My wife did everything in her power to find out what was going on with our son.

It took almost three years to finally get the diagnosis of autism. Our love and commitment to this beautiful child would consume much of our marriage trying to figure out what was best for his development. My wife fought hard with doctors and the educational system. She was so focused and educated herself on medications and clinical trials such as leaky gut syndrome. I admired her strength and endless pursuits to give our son the best quality of life possible.

As he continued to mature, our challenges became more difficult. I focused on protecting my son, my wife, and my other children from the aggression that our beautiful boy couldn't control. There was many a day spent trying to protect him from hurting himself or those around him. My wife was petite, and I was always worried about her safety. She worked feverishly trying to accommodate our son's needs and trying to figure out what medications would work best. My job was to protect my boy and his surroundings while my wife dealt with his behavior issues and educational needs. She was a wealth of knowledge.

Weekend visits with my other children were a joy. They tried to understand the challenges facing their brother. They love their brother for who he is. He is their brother and they show love and compassion, understanding his special needs and circumstances. They help him with whatever makes him happy. I am so very proud of each of them. My boy loved Barney the dinosaur, SpongeBob SquarePants, and the host of vacuum cleaners blanketing the basement storage area. Lawn tractors would enter the picture as well as CDs, laptops, and grills. This child is so smart. I wish more people understood this. His world is perceived differently but his intelligence is so amazing.

Life would continue to have its challenges. There would be financial difficulties and career changes. My wife gave me the courage to move on to better-paying jobs. I do not think that I would have been able to make those crucial decisions had it not been for her. I eventually ended up working for a school district as director of facilities, a rewarding job that would help sustain us. I loved this position and worked there for twenty-two years before retiring.

As for my marriage, it did not last. There is that stigma out there. Married couples that have special needs children always end up divorced. I did not want to be one of those statistics. We were married for twenty-five years. I honestly did not see it coming. I was focused on providing for the family and the needs of our son. My other children were doing well in their education and their futures looked very bright. My love for my wife never diminished but I may have lost sight of my priorities. My son was my focus. I always stayed home after work and was not interested in doing anything else but being with him.

My wife worked a lot of hours in the evening, so we didn't see much of one another. It never dawned on me that we would drift apart because I loved her so deeply. All I know is that she eventually fell out of love with me. I lived in denial for some time. The pain of losing the person that I loved more than life itself became a reality.

The divorce crushed me. She remarried and each night when I kneel before God now, I continue to pray that she is happy. Her husband is good to my son and I am thankful for that; he is a good man. His love for her and my son is evident in his selfless actions. They love my son and one another and their happiness is all that matters to me now. I want her to feel loved.

When she remarried, I decided to check out dating sites. I met a woman that showered me with rose petals and a sexual experience that I was not prepared for. She was amazing. She understood my past. The demons that I have shared with you, she understood, and blessed me with love and experiences that helped me process my divorce and childhood trauma. I would see her on weekend visits for four and a half years, only to have it end because of our differences in distance and family circumstances. I miss her deeply and pray that she is doing well. I am so grateful for her love and support. She helped me through a very difficult time in my life and I often wonder if we had continued in our relationship, would we be happy together? I also pray for her each night. What a blessing. Thank you, Lord, for this intervention in my life.

After publishing my first book I was overwhelmed by the loving responses from my children, friends, and coworkers. I can't imagine how I would have reacted after reading a book based on the person that I worked side by side with on a daily basis. As I mentioned, I worked for a school district and many teachers, staff, and employees working under me read it. They would never in a million years have guessed that I had a past such as this. My character and work ethic shrouded my past so well that there was not a hint of darkness revealed.

I found myself immersed in personal conversations with so many people. The book brought their hidden demons to light and we shared many secrets. We were able to connect because we had something in common, something that needed to come out, something that could no longer hold us. What an awesome experience! This was the reason I published my first book. I wanted to help others that were struggling to open up and let it out. As for my children, they love their dad and understand him. They are very proud of my accomplishments and support me in any way possible. Talk about being blessed!

Another wonderful blessing as a result of publishing the book was reuniting with my foster brother Rudy. I was sitting in the living room of the group home where my beautiful boy lives, talking about my adventures in Summersville, when one of the workers asked what foster home I lived in. My foster mother Loretta, who lived in Summersville, was somehow related to her. She knew where Rudy was, and we found each other! We have been in contact ever since.

I enjoy Thanksgiving and Christmas dinners with Rudy and his family. We visit Summersville together and reminisce. Rudy is not my foster brother; he is my brother, my blood. We talk about our crazy antics and relive the fond memories that I so cherish. His wife, daughter, and granddaughter love to hear the stories and treat me with much love and kindness. I cannot leave their house without taking food home with me. I do not believe our reuniting was a coincidence.

REBECCA AND I

Below is an excerpt from my original book. It is a precursor to the meeting I had with my sister after publishing my first book. This section relates to my father and his knowledge of sexual abuse and my sister's response to my guilt and weakness. Guilt and weakness that I lived with for forty-seven years.

Several years into my marriage, I became reacquainted with my real father. He managed to locate where we lived and showed up one day out of the blue. My wife had an uneasy feeling about my father right from the start because of the way he acted towards our family. I didn't like the way he talked about our beautiful autistic boy. It was like he felt uneasy knowing that I had a special needs son that was part of his DNA. The topics were always about him. It reminded me of my childhood visits where he needed to be the main focus. He had found a woman that helped him get well and away from alcohol. I only met her and her children a handful of times. They were well-educated and had great jobs.

Dad (I feel uneasy saying the word) would stop by my house and visit only briefly. He would continue to drop by unannounced and my wife became frustrated because of this. I sensed that he showed interest in me because I had made something of myself. We would drive around in his new car so he could show it off to me. Clearly, he wanted me to see that he was living a good life with his new family. He took me to see his home and the backyard pool. We would eat a nice meal and talk about his stepchildren. He wanted me to feel proud of him. My children and my brothers and sisters were not part of the conversation unless I brought them into it.

I do not want to spend time dwelling on my real brothers' and sisters' lifestyles when they were adults because they had many hardships and did the best that they could as a result of how they were brought up. Not all my brothers and sisters were moved into foster care. The older siblings remained at home and had to deal with a father that drank and a mother that had psychological problems. I had very little contact with my siblings.

For some crazy reason I feel I need to share this. Remember when I talked about the pocketknives and little toys that my father would give me when I was three? Well, on two separate occasions, when he dropped me off after visiting, he reached into his glove compartment and gave me a tire-pressure gauge and then a can of bug removal! I took both. They sit in my garage today, thirty years later. Why?

It became very apparent to me that (at least as it relates to me and my children) we were considered the other family in my father's eyes. He had his new lifestyle and successful family, and that was what made him feel good. I guess I can understand to some extent why he would feel this way, but it still bothered me tremendously. My spouse pretty much figured this out right away. It took me a little longer because I was hoping to reconnect and have a meaningful relationship with him. That would never come about.

Then it happened … You would think that there would be no more paperwork to file in the vault. I was building a life of my own, far away from that house, though still haunted with demons and pretending to be normal. At least I was doing a good job at taking care of my family and working hard to keep my thoughts hidden. I was mistaken.

It was the typical drive followed by a sit-down meal. My father was sitting across from me and began to talk about my sister, Rebecca. I remember saying how happy I was that she left me and found a good foster home. I never spoke to him about the sexual abuse that William and I had endured. I never spoke to anyone about it! I was rambling about the one visit that I had at Rebecca's new foster home, how clean the house was, and all the pets when he stopped me. "Did you know the oldest boy made her suck on his penis?"

This was my little sister. I lost it! I knew that I had never told anyone! The person sitting in front of me was the father of this little girl. "What did you do when you found out?" I asked. "When did you find this out?" He said that Rebecca confronted Janet after she had moved into the new foster home but nothing ever came of it. "That was it? You never pursued it?"

I was in shock! Rebecca had left the foster home that we shared, and I stayed for many years after.

When did my real father find out? Why didn't he do anything about it? Did he know this while I was still in the home? I was so sick inside that I could barely function. I wanted to scream! All I could think about was my poor sister. Oh my God! I know what it was like having to do that. My sister was just a little child, barely six years old.

The time that we were sitting on the floorboards of the Volkswagen van came flooding back to me. Did the oldest boy do this to her? I have no proof. I never witnessed it or even thought about her being taken like I was. I thought that what had happened to me and William stayed with me and William and no one else.

I do not remember how I made it back to my driveway. It was all a blur. I lost all respect for my father after that and maintained very little contact with him. The fact that he did nothing to confront these people for my sister's sake devastated me. I let him go. My former spouse was right. He obviously cared little for his real family. He lived out the rest of his life in the south with his successful family. I only saw him twice. Phone conversations dwindled and faded away. When he passed away (on my birthday), I didn't go to his funeral.

I do not know if my sister confronted the Peters. I have not spoken to her about how I feel and how sorry I am for not protecting her. The guilt that I carry (especially the alleged sexual abuse) continues to plague me. I am still the coward. I do not speak to Rebecca. I only see her at funerals. I have no idea what she thinks of me. I love her deeply, yet I choose to stay away. We are getting older, and my fear is that I may take the unspoken words to my grave, never knowing her thoughts.

All that I have is the memories of a little girl who was terribly tormented and abused. She is my sister, and I have lost decades of contact. We never held each other. I live with the memories of chopped-up hair and red, swollen cheeks. I see her bound and gagged with urine flowing down her legs. I picture winter boots with no socks on a cold snowy day. I have terrible, terrible visions of what might have happened at the hands of the oldest boy. I sit typing these words, and I know when I stop, I will not call her. It is truly sad that I can do so many things and pretend to be something that I am not, yet I cannot do this.

Time is ticking away. There is only me, my sister Rebecca, and my oldest sister. All the others have died. Warren, Daniel, and Trisha are gone, and my mother passed away many years ago. Dad is gone too.

THE MEETING

After publishing my first book, I met with my sister. I had looked up her phone number previously when I told her about the book because I wanted her to read it. I needed to reflect on my forty-seven years of guilt. She agreed to meet me for a bite to eat and visit my home. The dinner at a local diner was nothing compared to the meeting at my home, just a few minutes from our dinner engagement. When I looked into my sister's eyes, someone that haunted my dreams, I discovered a person of unbelievable strength who not only forgave me of my weakness, but found no fault in my actions. She understood the circumstances. We were just little children that were taken advantage of in unspeakable ways. We had no control. I could argue the fact that I denied the abuse, but she knew the fear of the consequences I envisioned in my mind were real to me.

Rebecca bought my book from one of the online print-on-demand services. Reading it immediately brought a page from her vault to the surface. She was reading about my circumstances because that is what the book does; it retrieves pages from the vault. This is what it is doing to many of you as you read it. I asked her about her response to my alleged sexual abuse account. She was very upset because she said she *was* sexual abused, nothing alleged about it, even though I never witnessed it.

She told me about a walk hand in hand with the foster father and the oldest boy to the bathroom located on the second level. The foster father and the oldest boy took this innocent six-year-old girl into the bathroom to perform oral sex. I immediately envisioned the walk. I played it in my mind as if I was watching a movie. I could see them, I could see her, I could see the surroundings, the hallway, the door to the third level, the bedroom that housed gags, restraints, and urine. Then the unimaginable vision of performing oral sex on two adults shut me down.

She needed to share this with me because of what she read in my first book. *There was sexual abuse.* I immediately understood her discontent. I had never considered the foster father in the equation. Opening this new chapter was beyond my comprehension. What ungodly trauma was about to be unveiled! She fell silent. She had made peace with her demons and I was not going to upset what worked for her. I must admit that my sister is much stronger than me. Rebecca found comfort in the foster family that loved her for who she was and to this day, considers them her mom and dad. Wow! What a blessing!

Rebecca has worked steadily throughout her life. In the beginning she struggled with alcoholism, but she didn't fall into self-pity. I find her strength in life's struggles and childhood trauma a testimony to her forgiving nature. My sister did not hold me accountable for her childhood trauma. Forty-seven years of guilt is hard to let go but when I looked into her eyes, I felt love, not blame. I lived most of my adult life feeling ashamed, as though I failed her, yet she set me free. What a beautiful woman.

Rebecca and I communicate on Facebook now. I find it fascinating to see that she has faith in God. I think Rebecca discovered the same thing that saved me. Only God can take a test and turn it into a testimony. She has a wonderful sense of humor. Rebecca has worked hard all her life and I know that the demons in her past still dwell within her. She has control though; she is strong and has mastered the enemy created by a broken system.

I love my sister and am proud of her. I am grateful for her forgiveness and I find it so sad that I waited almost five decades to receive it. I still struggle with guilt, but she has helped me understand my inability as a child to protect her.

THE POWER IN MY WEAKNESS

Weakness is defined as "the state or condition of lacking strength." I have always been strong physically. I will be sixty-two in a month and I can still bench press two hundred and forty pounds. I only weigh one hundred and forty-five pounds. I was, however, a person harboring tremendous guilt, shame, self-pity, low self-esteem, a person in denial, in fear of loss, in fear of love, anxious in being unsuccessful, lacking in trust or to be trusted, afraid to let go, afraid in being let go, wanting to be loved yet not knowing the true meaning of love, afraid of giving, uneasy in receiving and not knowing how to express my feelings appropriately.

I have full control over my physical being. Picking up weights and straining my body to the point of hypertrophy is an awesome feeling, especially when you can see the results. When I look at myself outwardly, I can say, *hey, I am doing pretty good for an old man.* I eat decently, take my protein and multivitamins, walk, workout, and at the end of the day, yes, physically I am good.

Then there is that long list that makes up what is happening on the inside, my soul, my subconscious, my mind, and my heart. Not so easy to control. We as human beings have the amazing ability to absorb and store everything that we see, feel, touch, or smell. We store it but may not be able to retrieve it when we want to. For example: I walk by a person that is wearing a perfume that I immediately recognize and boom! I am brought back to a scene that gives me goose bumps. This is not a coincidence; it is the mind triggering an actual event that took place many years ago. Sometimes it is warm and wonderful and sometimes it is the skunk cabbage that brings back a scene that is not so pleasant.

We are a product of our past experiences. I cannot tell you how many times I have heard people say "forget about the past, it can't hurt you now." I can understand that the past cannot coexist in the present. Every time I press down on the keyboard, times past cannot be retrieved. I get that.

But every word or sentence as you have read this book has just become part of your past that has been embedded in your mind and which may affect you in some way in the future. Friends, what I am trying to say is literally everything that has happened to you or me from birth (even prior to birth) to this very second makes you who you are today, at this very moment. There is no erasing the past. There is no "you need to forget about the past" or "just remember the good things" that brought you joy. That litany of words describing my inner being, well, that is a product of my past. It is not a product of my present. There is no need to include the future because we haven't learned anything from that yet, have we? You can only apply what you have learned from the past to affect the present and what you may decide to do in the future because of it.

So now what, Jacob, you may ask? We are a product of our past, the good and the bad, so what? If you say, "I read this story and believe me, this is nothing compared to what I went through," I want to say how deeply sorry I am for your suffering. I understand at least to some extent how you feel because I know what trauma does to a person, especially a child. I hope that you find peace and I pray that you continue reading this until the end.

Let's look at what our past is made up of. It is all about what we choose to do or not do by responding to what those that we interact with choose to do or not do to us. God has given us the gift of free will. It is what we do with that gift that makes all the difference; it is that simple. You didn't choose to be born. That was a choice given by your parents. Even an unplanned pregnancy is a choice. Both my partner and I chose to have sex without protection. A child was born based upon that decision. Both were choices, both produced the same outcome, a beautiful, completely helpless child. A child brought into this world that relied on the love and support of his or her parents. Life begins.

Choices will always result in consequences. It is part of being human. It is what life is based upon. We choose to get up, we choose to go to work, we choose to have dinner with family. I chose to be silent. We base our everyday decisions on the outcomes of our past experiences. What is important is that we learn from them in a positive way. We can even learn from witnessing or reading about other people's choices, like the people in this book.

So, Jacob, "where is the power in your weakness"? After reading the abundance of issues that I personally dealt with, you would think that there is no hope. Well, we are back to choices, or more importantly the gift of free will. There is certainly no power in any of these issues if you look at them separately and in definition. There are coping mechanisms. Alcohol, drugs, prescription pills, porn, adultery, or binge eating. I am sure that there are many more. None of these mechanisms are associated with power or strength; they are simply a way to cope.

It's sad that so many people live this way because the choices that others have made have affected their way of thinking, damaging their thought processes, and programing their future in a negative way. I must admit that my early drinking days were helping me keep the vault in check. My sister fought that battle too. I have been on several antidepressants in the past that did little as far as providing a coping mechanism. They did help me sleep! I have been to therapy and it did help some. It helped me to realize that talking to someone about (the least embarrassing) of my dark secrets helped. Then the breakthrough came.

When you are divorced and living alone you have a lot of time to think. I decided to put down on paper what was lurking deep inside my brain. Why was I at this point in my life? I had lost my beautiful wife and my autistic son was transitioned into a group home. I was sitting alone in a big house that was now on the market. I wanted to just move away to a place that could help me distance myself from the memories of the house I was sitting in. Silly thinking because those memories will go with me.

I had also lost a dear friend. He was a priest that always gave me good advice. We spent twenty-three years going out to dinner on Friday night. I loved our fish-fry season.

Anyway, I started to think about my life and what went wrong. I started from the beginning and wrote it down on paper, thinking, *well, at least I can pull everything out of the vault and see it.* As I did this, I began to realize that writing things down on paper is a good thing. I started to understand why I was feeling so lost. I started to connect my weaknesses with my strength or power. According to the dictionary, the definition of power is "the ability to do something or act in a particular way, especially as a faculty or quality." I began to think about the way I act. The endless chores that I was forced to do helped me.

I used to think that I was nothing but a slave, weak, cowardly and adhering to every command so I wouldn't be punished. Had I not complied there would have been serious consequences so yes, that was the driving factor. However, this rigorous routine that was not meant for a child ultimately helped me in my career. It taught me to be neat, meticulous, focused, task-oriented, time-structured, adhere to specific orders, be respectful of superiors, and yes, comply. That is eight powerful abilities. I must admit that my OCD when it comes to cleaning did affect my relationships. I have calmed down a bit but if you were to visit my home, you could eat off the floors.

The pain and suffering that I witnessed and my inability to defend others, the tremendous guilt, were the driving factors that kept my vault sealed as much as possible. They were also the hardest thing for me to suppress. I consider the inability to protect and the harboring of guilt to be the greatest defeat in my childhood experience. It is what birthed this book.

How does this give me power, you may ask? It seems impossible, right? Well, when I looked into my sisters' eyes that were so focused on her captor as she was being force-fed and beaten, I felt deep sorrow and my heart ached. My mind understood her suffering. It allowed me to grasp the concept of evil and what it does to a person.

There are two ways to feel pain. The first is the pain that we feel when someone is attacking our physical body. The second, and for me the most profound, is witnessing the pain and suffering of someone without the ability to intervene. You can see the outward effects of what pain and suffering does; how people react; how they cower; how the tears flow; how the body reacts to every blow; the haunting look on their faces; eyes that are so focused, it pierces the soul; and the ultimate feeling of helplessness. Today, this experience is what gives me the ability to connect and feel deep compassion for those that I come across in life that are struggling, even those that I have no association with. I understand their suffering and pray for them. I know that this is a result of the trauma in my childhood. I am more loving and compassionate because of it. Yes, my friends, there is power in my weakness.

I still have dreams. They pop up now and then. Some are so bizarre and terribly disgusting that I have to wonder if I should make a phone call to my counselor just so we can try and figure it out. This is normal. It will happen until the day I die. I just contemplate the meaning and let it go!

I would like to share why, after so many years of struggling with my inner turmoil, I am at peace. Some of you reading this may not believe in God. I respect all people, and your understanding of faith is yours and yours alone. For me, it started with taking what was in my head and putting it on paper. It took a bit, but I began to realize that God was with me all the time, even when I didn't know Him. A simple nightly prayer, the long walk to the church with a beautiful, loving foster mother, the only mother figure that I had in my entire childhood … I believe that's when the seed was planted in me. Then there was the dream that I was being held by God, when there was no predisposed knowledge of Him growing inside of me. I was too busy trying to survive. The discovery of the crucifix buried in the back of the closet, a crucifix that depicted suffering, somehow brought me comfort.

Tears are flowing from my eyes as I type this. I can feel His presence and it brings joy to my heart.

I am not alone. I am never alone. I have the gift of free will. I have knowledge of Him. I have read the Bible cover to cover and discovered that God uses our weaknesses in amazing ways to strengthen us, to strengthen those we encounter, to share the love of Jesus.

"My grace is sufficient for you, for my power I made perfect in weakness." That's 2 Corinthians 12:9. I love this passage. It verifies my thoughts and gives me the power to accept my suffering in a positive and loving way. Just reflect on what Jesus did. Despite all the miracles that He performed, He suffered by being beaten, scourged, nailed to a cross, and was exposed to the people as a human. In their minds, he was weak. He wasn't stepping down from the suffering; He had a purpose that He fulfilled just so those that believe in Him can be saved.

The comfort I felt when clinging to that crucifix now makes sense. I wasn't clinging to or worshiping an idol; I was clinging to a presence. I am so grateful that I studied with some wonderful Bible-believing people. We had differences in thought on occasion, but that is how we grow in the truth. Many of us believe in God when things are going well. When the bomb drops, that belief turns to blame. Blame?

Another one of my favorite scripture passages is "When under trial let no one say I am being tried by God. For with evil things God cannot be tried, nor does he himself try anyone." James 1:13.

God is blameless. That gift of free will that I keep coming back to, well, it is our responsibility to accept this powerful gift. It gives us the ability to decide our destiny. God cannot do evil, He is a loving God. Evil exists because of Satan and his influence on our beliefs. It all started with Adam, and Jesus was the final sacrifice to save those of us who believe. There was no other way. We as humans are not capable of adhering to the six hundred and thirteen Old Testament laws. We sin every day. The only way to everlasting life is to believe in Jesus Christ as your Lord and Savior!

Jesus was the final sacrifice that opened the door to God; the veil was torn. Through Jesus we can talk to our God! It is in this belief that we are saved. "For the righteous one may fall seven times, and he will get back up again, but the wicked will be made to stumble by calamity" Proverbs 24:16. A wonderful passage! I sin, but I can get back up because I know that God is forgiving and my belief in Jesus will keep me from condemnation.

"Love the Lord your God with all your heart and with all your soul and with all your mind" Matthew 22:37. The second commandment is to "love thy neighbor as thyself." If we try to live by these two commandments we will never have to worry about the highs and the lows because His grace is sufficient. Grace is an "unmerited favor—His goodness towards those who have no claim on, nor reason to expect, divine favor, salvation by grace. God's grace has been manifested in the form of a gift. We do not earn it. Nothing we do can affect His undeserved kindness.

There are many stories in the Bible that simply amazed me. Job, Jonah, Solomon, David, Noah, creation, and so many more. I fell in love with the Old

Testament. I can remember hearing stories while growing up that actually made me fear God. The falsehood that He will make you suffer if you do something wrong is so far from the truth. Thinking that way separates us from Him.

I went to church for many years, but I didn't learn anything compared to personal study. Church had its readings, but I grasped very little. I never sat and read the Bible so I couldn't connect with the true meaning. I didn't know if it was from the Old or the New Testament. I didn't connect with the history or places. I thought that going to church and spending time with my wonderful priest was what connected me with God. I still feared God and struggled with my sins, waiting for the retribution to come at any time. I didn't realize how far off I was from knowing the truth.

Studying the Bible opened my eyes. I do not claim to be proficient in scripture. I have difficulty in memorization, but I certainly retain its meaning. The only salvation is through my belief in what Jesus did for me, and for us.

I decided to share my faith and how it came about because all of us that suffer with our demons have a way out; we just don't know it. The actions, the choices, the inability to look beyond our circumstances and the daily struggle to exist separates us from the love of God and that is so sad. This book is about trauma and how it affects the mind of a child as he moves through life's struggles. Physical, emotional, and sexual abuse is a result of what one person chooses to do to another, God has nothing to do with it. But it is also about overcoming and finding peace.

I think most people find the truth later in life. I am one of those people. One of my favorite passages in scripture is in Romans 7:14-24. Paul, a righteous man who wrote thirteen New Testament books, acknowledges that he cannot live up to all that he preaches, yet in verse 25 he finds comfort in knowing he is saved through Jesus.

Paul was human. We are human and incapable of being perfect. God knew this so he sent Jesus to teach us, to die for us, and to rise again to break the bondage of death. There is life after death for those who believe.

So now I am free! My sister forgave me, and I have been able to forgive those that harmed me. I forgave my father and the choices that he made, a forgiveness that comes from my heart. I pray for those that harmed me in the foster homes, that they find Jesus. Who am I to judge? "Judge and ye shall be judged "Matthew 7:2. Why would I not want to see those people saved? Hate is a terrible trait and only Satan relishes in that. It is never too late. David had Uriah killed so he could have his wife. Paul feverishly sought to destroy the followers of Jesus. God used them to bring us closer to the ultimate gift. God will use our human weakness in ways that bring about good. He is at work in the darkness and the light.

Do I still struggle? Yes! Do I have negative thoughts? Yes! Do I fail in my relationship with God? Yes! I am human. I will never be perfect and there is no changing that. I am a sinner. I accept this. I also know that I am right with God because of my faith and belief in Jesus. I try very hard to be a loving and kind person. I try very hard to block out negative thoughts. I will struggle with this until I am taken. The very fact that I have the knowledge of truth, however, allows peace to enter my heart and mind. I find peace in the truth.

Friend, don't blame God for your troubles; look to Him for help. "You have not because you ask not "James 4:2. Read the Bible. Prayer is empty if you are praying without the knowledge of Jesus. He is the only avenue to God. Through Him you will find that prayer works because God is listening. Answers come in His time, not ours. Be patient. Your life will change in ways you never thought possible.

SO TODAY

So today, what have I to be thankful for? I live a life that I devote to God. I am single and live alone in a quiet country setting. There is no struggle in finding a mate. God will send someone my way, or He may not. I find comfort in Him. There are no worries in my heart. Should someone come my way, whether someone in my past or someone in my future, only God knows, and I trust in Him. I know that I am loved, a love that I will never have to worry about losing.

I hope this story comforts you and gives you strength in knowing that you are not alone. Physical, emotional, and sexual abuse is embedded in many of those reading this book. This is just one of many books that I pray will help you break the chains of silence. Don't wait forty-seven years like I did. Your story is just as important and I hope that you will take advantage of my story to help heal the scars associated with your own personal trauma.

Make the choice. Please let it out! Open the vault, put it down on paper, look at what you have written, and share it. Let it go. Turn your test into a testimony. Talk to someone! Talk to me! I am here for you. Google "author Jacob Matthews" and you will find me. You deserve better. You deserve to be loved. God loves you so much! I love you! **Find forgiveness,** my friend, and set yourself free!

Always and forever,
Jacob.
matthewsj1957@gmail.com

ABOUT THE AUTHOR

Life is a gift. It is a fleeting moment in time. Before we know it, we are barely able to stand. We look back at three generations and wonder how we got here. My time is fading. Did I make others in my life feel the love that they deserved or so desperately needed? Am I a product of my own making? Yes and no. I want to make a difference. I want to go out knowing that I did something good. Something that will help others in their struggles.

ABOUT THE BOOK

We all have our demons; those hidden secrets that stay tucked away in the recesses of our minds. We think we have control; we think we can keep them buried with no one ever discovering them. These secrets have a hold on us. They are a part of who we are and no matter what we try to do to keep them in check, we suffer, and we fail. There is hope available, my friend. Do you want to know peace? Open this book and read. You will find that you are not alone. You are never alone. Someone is with you, waiting patiently to set you free.

9 781642 379068